HE GAVE GIFTS UNTO MEN

A Biblical Perspective of Apostles, Prophets, and Pastors

Kenneth E. Hagin

First Edition
Third Printing 1994

ISBN 0-89276-517-8

In the U.S. write:
Kenneth Hagin Ministries
P.O. Box 50126
Tulsa, OK 74150-0126

In Canada write:
Kenneth Hagin Ministries
P.O. Box 335
Etobicoke (Toronto), Ontario
Canada, M9A 4X3

BOOKS BY KENNETH E. HAGIN

* Redeemed From Poverty, Sickness and Spiritual Death
* What Faith Is
* Seven Vital Steps To Receiving the Holy Spirit
* Right and Wrong Thinking
  Prayer Secrets
* Authority of the Believer (foreign only)
* How To Turn Your Faith Loose
  The Key to Scriptural Healing
  Praying To Get Results
  The Present-Day Ministry of Jesus Christ
  The Gift of Prophecy
  Healing Belongs to Us
  The Real Faith
  How You Can Know the Will of God
  Man on Three Dimensions
  The Human Spirit
  Turning Hopeless Situations Around
  Casting Your Cares Upon the Lord
  Seven Steps for Judging Prophecy
* The Interceding Christian
  Faith Food for Autumn
* Faith Food for Winter
  Faith Food for Spring
  Faith Food for Summer
* New Thresholds of Faith
* Prevailing Prayer to Peace
* Concerning Spiritual Gifts
  Bible Faith Study Course
  Bible Prayer Study Course
  The Holy Spirit and His Gifts
* The Ministry Gifts (Study Guide)
  Seven Things You Should Know About Divine Healing
  El Shaddai
  Zoe: The God-Kind of Life
  A Commonsense Guide to Fasting
  Must Christians Suffer?
  The Woman Question
  The Believer's Authority
  Ministering to Your Family
  What To Do When Faith Seems Weak and Victory Lost
  Growing Up, Spiritually
  Bodily Healing and the Atonement
  Exceedingly Growing Faith
  Understanding the Anointing
  I Believe in Visions
  Understanding How To Fight the Good Fight of Faith
  Plans, Purposes, and Pursuits
  How You Can Be Led by the Spirit of God
  A Fresh Anointing
  The Art of Prayer
  Classic Sermons

He Gave Gifts Unto Men:
    A Biblical Perspective of Apostles, Prophets, and Pastors
The Price Is Not Greater Than God's Grace (Mrs. Oretha Hagin)

MINIBOOKS (A partial listing)

* The New Birth
* Why Tongues?
* In Him
* God's Medicine
* You Can Have What You Say
  How To Write Your Own Ticket With God
* Don't Blame God
* Words
  Plead Your Case
* How To Keep Your Healing
  The Bible Way To Receive the Holy Spirit
  I Went to Hell
  How To Walk in Love
  The Precious Blood of Jesus
* Love Never Fails
  Learning To Flow With the Spirit of God
  The Glory of God
  Hear and Be Healed
  Knowing What Belongs to Us
  Your Faith in God Will Work

BOOKS BY KENNETH HAGIN JR.

* Man's Impossibility — God's Possibility
  Because of Jesus
  How To Make the Dream God Gave You Come True
  The Life of Obedience
  God's Irresistible Word
  Healing: Forever Settled
  Don't Quit! Your Faith Will See You Through
  The Untapped Power in Praise
  Listen to Your Heart
  What Comes After Faith?

MINIBOOKS (A partial listing)

* Faith Worketh by Love
  Blueprint for Building Strong Faith
* Seven Hindrances to Healing
* The Past Tense of God's Word
  Faith Takes Back What the Devil's Stolen
  "The Prison Door Is Open — What Are You Still Doing Inside?"
  How To Be a Success in Life
  Get Acquainted With God
  Showdown With the Devil
  Unforgiveness
  Ministering to the Brokenhearted

*These titles are also available in Spanish. Information about other foreign translations of several of the above titles (i.e., Finnish, French, German, Indonesian, Polish, Russian, Norwegian, Portuguese, Korean, Japanese, Chinese Mandarin, etc.) may be obtained by writing to: Kenneth Hagin Ministries, P.O. Box 50126, Tulsa, Oklahoma 74150-0126.

Contents

Preface

Jesus Christ, the Head of the Church, is getting His Body ready for His soon return. That's why it is vital for those who are called to the ministry to function in their proper place in the Body of Christ.

Some controversy has arisen in our day about the roles of the apostle and prophet in the Body of Christ. Some believers purport that these offices do not even exist today. Others take a radical viewpoint concerning the authority these offices hold in the local church over the pastor and over believers in general.

This book is a scriptural look at the offices of the apostle, prophet, and pastor as they are to function in the Body of Christ today. These offices have never been taken out of the Body of Christ, but I believe God wants to bring biblical balance to this area of teaching.

SECTION I

APOSTLES

Chapter 1
Ranks or Classes of Apostles

. . . When he [Jesus] ascended up on high, he led captivity captive, and GAVE GIFTS UNTO MEN. . . .

And he [Jesus] GAVE some, APOSTLES; and some, prophets; and some, evangelists; and some, pastors and teachers.

— Ephesians 4:8,11

And God HATH SET SOME IN THE CHURCH, first APOSTLES, secondarily prophets, thirdly teachers, after that miracles, then gifts of healings, helps, governments, diversities of tongues.

— 1 Corinthians 12:28

Ministry Gifts: A *Divine* Call

Five ministry gifts are mentioned in Ephesians 4:11. A ministry gift is resident within a person who is called by God to the full-time ministry to stand in one of these five ministry offices: apostle, prophet, evangelist, pastor, and teacher.

Some people say that all the ministry gifts operate in the Church today except the offices of the apostle and the prophet. But where in Scripture does it say that God ever took those offices out of the Church or that the Church no longer needs these ministry gifts?

Paul wrote this epistle to the Ephesians many years after the Church had its beginnings. So if God had taken the offices of the apostle and prophet out of the Church, Paul would have said, "God gave *evangelists* and *pastors* and *teachers* to the Church." But he didn't say that. God gave all five ministry gifts to the Church, and they have never ceased functioning. They are all in operation even in our day.

The Bible tells us why and for how long the ministry gifts were given to the Church.

> **EPHESIANS 4:12,13**
> **12 For the perfecting of the saints, for the work of the ministry, for the edifying of the body of Christ:**
> **13 Till we all come in the unity of the faith, and of the knowledge of the Son of God, unto a perfect** [spiritually mature] **man, unto the measure of the stature of the fulness of Christ.**

These verses tell us three reasons ministry gifts were given to the Church:

1. For the perfecting of the saints.

2. For the work of the ministry.

3. For the edifying of the Body of Christ.

Actually, the Greek indicates that the meaning is "perfecting of the saints so the saints can do the work of the ministry, resulting in the edification of the Body of Christ."

Another translation says that God gave the fivefold ministry gifts "in order to get His holy people ready to serve as workers" (*The New Testament in the Language of Today*, William F. Beck). The *Godspeed* translation says God gave ministry gifts to the Church so the saints can "reach mature manhood, and reach that measure of development found in Christ."

How long will ministry gifts be in the Church? Ephesians 4:13 says, *"Till we all come in the unity of the faith, and of the knowledge of the Son of God, unto a perfect* [spiritually mature] *man, unto the measure of the stature of the fulness of Christ."*

Don't let the words "perfecting" and "perfect" in verses 12 and 13 throw you. We will never be perfect or perfected in the flesh. As long as we are in these mortal bodies, we will not reach perfection in the sense that most people think of perfection. Actually, the word "perfect" here means *mature* or *full manhood*. The Bible is talking about *spiritual maturity*.

The Church will always need ministry gifts — those called to the offices of apostle, prophet, evangelist, pastor, and teacher — because as a body of believers, we are always in the process of growing toward the full stature of Christ. Even when Jesus returns, there will be those in the Body of Christ who just got saved and are still spiritual babes.

There is an anointing that goes with every one of these fivefold ministry offices. And as ministers of God stand in these different offices, the anointing of the Holy Spirit is distributed in different measures and works differently in each office. But all the ministry gifts are for the edifying or the spiritual building up of the Body of Christ.

There is an anointing upon each ministry gift — the full-time minister — that is *not* on the layman. No layman can take the place of these ministry gifts that God has set in the Church. Of course, laymen can witness for God and do much to further the growth of God's Kingdom. And in that general sense, everyone is in the ministry to serve as workers in the Body of Christ.

But the ministry gifts are those people called to the full-time ministry, who are anointed by God to help equip and mature the saints. Unless we have the manifestation and operation of these ministry gifts in the Church, the saints will not mature, nor be equipped as they should to do the work of the ministry.

Notice something else about the ministry gifts. In Ephesians 4:11, it says that Jesus *gave* these ministry gifts unto men. In First Corinthians 12:28, it says that God *set* the ministry gifts into the Church. *God* gave ministry gifts to man, and *God* set them in the Church — not man. There is a vast difference.

You do not enter any phase of the ministry just because you want to, because someone told you to, or because someone prophesied to you. No man calls you to the ministry; it is a *divine* call. God alone *sets* men and women into ministry gift offices.

Those whom God calls *to* the ministry, He equips *for* the ministry. God anoints those called to the ministry and gives them the *spiritual ability* to stand in whatever office He calls them to.

As important as education and ambition are to success, we need more than education or ambition if we are going to be successful in the ministry. We need a ministry equipped with supernatural gifts — supernatural *equipment*.

The ministry consists not in *name*, but in the *power* that the Lord Jesus Christ, the Head of the Church, bestows upon a person to stand in a ministry office. I get amused at folks who go around calling themselves by certain titles. Putting a label on something doesn't make it so. You can put a label on an empty can, but that doesn't put anything in the can!

The Bible says the Lord Jesus Christ Himself *gave* ministry gifts to the Body of Christ. Yet some people presumptuously go around laying hands on others, supposedly putting them into these different ministry offices. That's impossible! I call it laying empty hands on empty heads! And it causes a problem in the Body of Christ because it encourages people to intrude into ministry offices for which they have no anointing and to which they have not been called.

Friends, you can't intrude into a ministry office that you are not called to by God. It is dangerous to do so. It could cost you your life. I have seen ministers die young because they didn't do what God told them to do and tried to intrude into ministry offices to which they were not called.

No one can "put" anyone else in a ministry office. God alone *sets* people into these offices. Other people may recognize and acknowledge such a calling, but it is God who calls and sets these ministry gifts in the Church.

Sometimes you hear people say, "I want to work for God, but I don't know whether or not I'm called." If you don't know whether or not you are called to the ministry, you probably are not. You see, if you have the *preach* or *teach* in you, it's going to come out. You don't have to teach a rooster to crow; he just crows because it's in him! And if the preach or teach is in you, it's going to come out.

Some people say, "I didn't have any call to the ministry. I just saw a need, so I fulfilled that need." Well, that might be true, but that doesn't put a person into one of these ministry offices.

Actually, each of us should be able to minister to others. And there is a general sense, of course, in which every Christian is a preacher. Every layman ought to be a preacher because to preach means to *proclaim* or to *tell* the good news of the gospel.

But that still does not qualify a person to stand in one of these ministry offices. To enter a ministry office requires a *divine* call. God gives the divine *call* to the ministry; He bestows the spiritual *equipment* for the ministry; and He requires certain *qualifications* of those in the ministry.

The particular method by which God calls one to the ministry is unimportant. What is important is a person's obedience to the call of God.

Divinely Granted Appearance

In 1987 I had a visitation from the Lord. The Lord

Jesus Christ appeared to me and talked to me. The entire experience lasted two hours and fifty minutes. Some of the things the Lord talked to me about in that visitation are found in the book, *Plans, Purposes, and Pursuits.*

In that visitation, Jesus talked to me about His plan for the New Testament Church, and how His plan for the Church in worship is different under the New Covenant than it was under the Old Covenant.

Then He began to talk to me about some of His plans for the Church concerning ministry. His plan for the Church in ministry is also different under the New Covenant than it was under the Old Covenant. And in this discussion, He began to talk to me about the *ministry gifts* that He has set in the Church.

In this book, I'm going to share with you some of the differences in Jesus' plan for the *ministry* under the New Covenant, especially regarding the offices of the apostle, prophet, and pastor.

Shortly after the 1987 visitation, it seemed that controversy arose in different parts of the Body of Christ, particularly concerning the offices of the apostle and the prophet. Of course, Jesus knew the doctrinal errors that were about to surface in the Church. I believe He addressed these issues in order to maintain balance and to help keep ministers from getting in a ditch doctrinally.

You see, there is an element of truth in all doctrinal error. Usually the error occurs when people push biblical truths to the extreme. Actually, there has to be an ele-

ment of truth involved in these spiritual tangents or no
one would believe them; the error would be too obvious.

I'm against the extreme on any issue. People can
even be extreme regarding faith. That's why I encourage people not to get into the ditch — into extremes and
excesses — in any area. Just stay right in the middle of
the road. Many of these errors about the offices of the
apostle and the prophet are due to lack of correct teaching in this area.

In the 1987 visitation, Jesus began talking about
the office of the apostle. He said, "There are four classes
or ranks of apostles. And within these different classes
or ranks, apostles can have different degrees or measures of anointing."

Jesus continued, "There are not only different
classes of apostles, but there are also different classes
of prophets, evangelists, pastors, and teachers. And
there are different degrees of anointings within these
different classes."

I think we have all seen people in these various
offices, ministering under varying degrees of anointing.
Even in the pastoral office, some pastors carry a different type or measure of anointing than others. And we
see evangelists, prophets, and teachers with different
degrees of anointing upon them. The same thing is true
in the apostolic office.

First Class of Apostle: Jesus Christ

Of course, Jesus stands at the Head of the list in

each of the fivefold ministry gifts.

The Bible calls Jesus an *apostle*. The Greek word translated "apostle" also means *a messenger, a sent one*, or *a commissioned one*. Hebrews 3:1 says, *". . . consider the APOSTLE and High Priest of our profession, Christ Jesus."*

Jesus certainly was commissioned, wasn't He? Jesus stands at the Head of the list of sent ones. He is called an Apostle because in His earthly ministry He was a *Sent One*, a *Messenger*, and a *Commissioned One* to bring the good news of salvation to the world.

Then Jesus called Himself a *prophet* (Matt. 13:57). He also stood in the *evangelist's* office because He proclaimed the good news of salvation (Luke 19:10). Jesus was a *pastor*; He called Himself the Good Shepherd (John 10:11-16). And He was a *teacher*; one of the main facets of Jesus' ministry was teaching people (Matt. 9:35).

Jesus is in a class by Himself in each ministry gift. No one else will ever stand in that highest class because Jesus had the Spirit without measure (John 3:34). No other person ever has, nor ever will be anointed *without* measure. Believers have the Spirit *by* measure (Rom. 12:3).

To say it another way, Jesus had a *degree of anointing* upon Him in His earthly ministry that no one else will ever have. Believers have *a measure* of that same anointing on them because they have the Holy Spirit. And it seems probable that the Body of Christ *as a whole* has the same measure of anointing Jesus had upon Him when He was upon the earth. But certainly no other individual has ever been or ever will be anointed to the same degree or in the same measure as Jesus was.

This is not to confuse the issue of Jesus' deity. As a Person Himself, Jesus was the eternal Son of God, the second member of the Trinity. He was God the Son, manifested in the flesh. But when He came to this earth, He emptied Himself of all divine privileges (Phil. 2:5-8) and ministered as a man.

In taking upon Himself a human nature, Jesus chose to surrender the independent exercise of His divine powers. At no time did Jesus ever cease being Deity, but He functioned as man anointed by the Holy Spirit.

We can understand this further by realizing that Jesus, before His incarnation, existed co-equally and co-eternally with God the Father and God the Holy Spirit. He shared with them all the privileges of deity, such as omniscience (being all-knowing), omnipotence (being all-powerful), and omnipresence (being everywhere at once).

When Jesus became the Babe of Bethlehem, He was Emmanuel, which means "God with us." He was God manifested in the flesh. He never ceased being God, nor did He lose His divinity, but He did lay aside certain privileges of deity and restricted Himself to certain human limitations.

Although Jesus was divine and sinless, He did not function as one who was omniscient. Rather, He *grew* in wisdom (Luke 2:52). He did not function as one who was omnipotent; He said He could of His own self do nothing

(John 5:19,30). He no longer functioned as one who was omnipresent, but was confined to a human body which later was nailed to the Cross and gloriously resurrected in the fulfilling of God's redemptive plan.

So Jesus never ceased being Deity, but He chose to come to the earth as a Man, and He ministered under the power and anointing of the Holy Spirit. But because He had the Spirit without measure (John 3:34), Jesus stands alone in a class by Himself in all five of the ministry gifts, including the office of the apostle.

In the 1987 visitation, Jesus went on to tell me about the other classes or ranks of apostles.

Second Class of Apostles: Apostles of the Lamb

The twelve Apostles of the Lamb are in the second class of apostles. Jesus said to me, "The Apostles of the Lamb are in a class by themselves. No one else can ever be in that class because there are no more Apostles of the Lamb."

In the Book of Revelation, the Word of God talks about the twelve Apostles of the Lamb.

REVELATION 21:14
14 And the wall of the city had twelve FOUNDA-TIONS, and in them the names of the twelve APOSTLES OF THE LAMB.

There are only twelve Apostles of the Lamb. And no one except the twelve apostles who companied with Jesus will ever stand in that second class of apostle. No one else could stand in that second class because the Apostles of the Lamb were *sent ones* for a specific time and purpose.

For what purpose were those twelve apostles *sent ones*? Were they sent to govern churches? Emphatically, no! They were sent ones to be eyewitnesses of Jesus' life, earthly ministry, and resurrection. We see this in the Scriptures.

Qualifications of the Apostles of the Lamb

ACTS 1:15-22

15 And in those days Peter stood up in the midst of the disciples, and said, (the number of names together were about an hundred and twenty,)

16 Men and brethren, this scripture must needs have been fulfilled, which the Holy Ghost by the mouth of David spake before concerning Judas, which was guide to them that took Jesus.

17 For he was numbered with us, and had obtained part of this ministry.

18 Now this man purchased a field with the reward of iniquity; and falling headlong, he burst asunder in the midst, and all his bowels gushed out.

19 And it was known unto all the dwellers at Jerusalem; insomuch as that field was called in their proper tongue, Aceldama, that is to say, The field of blood.

20 For it is written in the book of Psalms, Let his habitation be desolate, and let no man dwell therein: and his bishoprick let another take.

21 Wherefore of these men [notice the qualifications] **WHICH HAVE COMPANIED WITH US ALL THE TIME THAT THE LORD JESUS WENT IN AND**

OUT AMONG US,
22 BEGINNING FROM THE BAPTISM OF JOHN,
UNTO THAT SAME DAY THAT HE WAS TAKEN UP
from us [Jesus' resurrection], must one be
ORDAINED to be a WITNESS [or eyewitness] WITH
US OF HIS RESURRECTION.

The first and most obvious characteristic of the
Apostles of the Lamb is that they were *ministers of the
gospel*. That means they were first and foremost
preachers and teachers of the Word.

Second, we notice they were men who had ". . . *companied with us all the time that the Lord Jesus went in
and out among us*" (v. 21). They had to be eyewitnesses
of Jesus' earthly ministry.

Third, the twelve Apostles of the Lamb had to be
sent ones for the purpose of being eyewitnesses of Jesus'
resurrection: ". . . *ordained to be a witness with us of his
resurrection*" (v. 22).

In other words, the Apostles of the Lamb had to be
men who were with Jesus during His earthly ministry
and had witnessed His resurrection. That is why the
twelve Apostles of the Lamb are in a class by themselves.

In the 1987 visitation, Jesus called this second class
of apostle — the Apostles of the Lamb — *foundational
apostles* because God used them to help lay down New
Testament doctrine (Eph. 2:20). And some of them
wrote various Books of the Bible.

You remember that when Judas betrayed Jesus, the
apostles had to select another man to take his place.
This man had to be someone who had been among them
and had also been an eyewitness of Jesus' ministry and

resurrection. Matthias was chosen to take Judas' place.

Some people say that when the apostles chose Matthias to take Judas' place, they missed God because Paul should have been chosen and included as an Apostle of the Lamb.

But Paul *couldn't* qualify as an Apostle of the Lamb because he was not an eyewitness of Jesus' ministry; Paul wasn't even born again when Jesus walked upon the earth. Paul didn't go in and out and company with Jesus and His disciples during the three years of Jesus' earthly ministry. And Paul was not an eyewitness of Jesus' resurrection.

There are also those who say that there were only twelve apostles and that the apostolic office ceased with those twelve apostles. In other words, they say that the Apostles of the Lamb are all the apostles there ever will be in the Body of Christ.

But go back and read the New Testament again, and you'll find that there were approximately twenty people called apostles or "sent ones." (For further study on this subject, see Rev. Kenneth E. Hagin's book, *The Ministry Gifts*.) Therefore, the office of the apostle did not cease with the Apostles of the Lamb.

Third Class of Apostle: Other Foundational Apostles

The third class of apostle is the rank or class of apostle that Paul was in. A characteristic of apostles in this class is that they also helped lay the doctrinal foundation of the New Testament.

In the 1987 visitation, Jesus also said to me, "Foundational apostles are found in the *second* and *third* class of apostles. Apostles and prophets of that rank or level were anointed to lay down the doctrine of the New Testament."

Apostles and prophets of the second and third class are to be considered *foundational* apostles and prophets because the gospel of the New Testament was revealed to them.

Paul was in that third class of foundational New Testament apostles and prophets. He wrote a large portion of the New Testament, and he wasn't taught the revelation of the mystery of Christ by man; he received it from the Holy Spirit.

> **EPHESIANS 3:4,5**
> 4   Whereby, when ye read, ye may understand MY KNOWLEDGE IN THE MYSTERY OF CHRIST,
> 5   Which in other ages was not made known unto the sons of men, as it is now REVEALED unto his holy APOSTLES and PROPHETS by the Spirit.

Paul preached the revelation of the gospel to the early New Testament saints, so we don't need to lay any other foundation. We only need to build upon the foundation which has already been laid for us in the New Testament.

> **EPHESIANS 2:19,20**
> 19 Now therefore ye are no more strangers and foreigners, but fellowcitizens with the saints, and

of the household of God;
20 And are BUILT UPON THE FOUNDATION OF
THE APOSTLES AND PROPHETS, Jesus Christ
himself being the chief corner stone.

The Church — the Body of Christ — is built on the
foundation that the apostles and prophets already laid
down for us in the New Testament. Now we are to *build*
on that foundation.

1 CORINTHIANS 3:10
10 According to the grace of God which is given
unto me, as a wise masterbuilder, I HAVE LAID
THE FOUNDATION, and another buildeth
thereon. But let every man take heed how he
buildeth thereupon.

No one is receiving additional revelation to *add* anything to the foundation of the gospel today, because we
already have the revelation of the New Testament.

Paul said, *"But though we, or an angel from heaven,
preach any other gospel unto you than that which we
have preached unto you, let him be accursed"* (Gal. 1:8).
Paul warned that we are to take heed how we build
upon the foundation that has already been laid (1 Cor.
3:10). We can't add to it or take away from it.

No Foundational Apostles Today

Then in the visitation, Jesus said something very
interesting to me. He said, "There are *no* foundational
apostles and *no* foundational prophets today. There are
no apostles or prophets today on the same *level* or

authority or in the same *rank* or with the same *degree of anointing* as the apostles and prophets of the Early Church. No one in the Church today is in the second or third class."

You see, when Jesus appeared to me in 1987, I didn't know exactly why He was explaining these things to me. But since Jesus talked to me in that visitation, I have become aware of errors surfacing in the Body of Christ, particularly on the issue of apostles and prophets. Then I could readily understand why Jesus Christ, the Head of the Church, discussed these major doctrinal issues at such length.

We will look at some of these modern-day errors in the light of the Scriptures.

First, some people today claim that in order to have proper New Testament church government, the fivefold ministry must operate in every local church and make up the *government* of each local church. (We'll discuss this error later in this book.)

Second, this erroneous teaching says that since apostles are listed first in the list of ministry gifts in Ephesians 4:11, that means they are preeminent over all the other ministry gifts. Supposing apostles are preeminent, some people assume that apostles should govern all the other ministry gifts in the local body, including the pastor.

Third, they teach that modern-day apostles and prophets are still supposed to be laying down New Testament doctrine and foundation. And they claim if you don't have an apostle governing your church and a prophet guiding your church, you don't have a correct New Testament foundation.

I believe this is why Jesus said so emphatically to me in the visitation, "There are *no* foundational apostles and prophets today." Jesus knew this error would be surfacing in the Body of Christ.

Jesus went on to explain that if there were apostles and prophets in our day who were on the same rank or level as Paul, for example, they could add to the doctrine of the New Testament.

You see, some folks today have gone to the extreme in what they teach about the apostolic office and have gotten off into error. In the first place, it is not scriptural that additional foundation has to be laid in the Church today.

Jesus Christ is the Chief Cornerstone. If we need apostles today to lay another foundation, then we need another cornerstone because the cornerstone is part of the foundation! You can see how absurd that is.

No, we have the same gospel, the same Christ, and the same foundation that was laid for us by the foundational apostles and prophets, and we are just building upon that sure foundation.

Think about it. You would never get a house built if you had to continually lay the foundation again and again. If you put the foundation in one week and took it out the next week to lay a new foundation, you'd never get the house built.

No, you've got to leave the foundation in place and keep building upon it. That's the reason Jesus told me there are no foundational apostles or prophets today; the foundation has been laid, and it is a sure foundation — one that the Church today can securely build upon.

Besides, no one in the Church today is even in the third class of apostle. If they were, they could add to the New Testament. But no one can because people today do not have the degree of anointing to stand in that office and to add additional doctrine to the Church.

Second, this doctrine is in error because it is erroneous to assume that apostles are listed first in Ephesians 4:11 and First Corinthians 12:28 because they are the most important ministry gift. They are *not* listed first to indicate that they are to rule over all the other ministry gifts. We need to understand how ministry gifts evolved in the Early Church to help us understand why Paul probably listed them in that order.

The Church in Infancy
And the Evolution of Ministry

By not rightly dividing the Word of God, some people have misrepresented the office of the apostle and taken it to the extreme. Anything taken to extreme is in error.

People need to interpret Scripture in the light of other Scripture on the same subject. Therefore, in order to rightly divide the Word of truth on any subject, people need to take all the scriptures on a given subject and study them in the light of all the Bible has to say on that subject.

By assuming the apostle is listed first because it is preeminent over all the other ministry gifts, some peo-

ple are going from church to church in a dictatorial attitude declaring that they are apostles and demanding
that people and churches submit to them.

Obviously, in the establishing of the *universal
Church* following the resurrection of Jesus, the apostles
and prophets were of primary importance because they
brought forth the revelation of the New Testament that
is the foundation upon which the Church in all genera-
tions is to be established.

However, in terms of the operation of the *local
church* today, First Corinthians 12:28 could not be
referring to the offices of apostles and prophets as the
most important offices or the governing offices with the
local church, because Paul listed governments as an
entirely separate category.

Therefore, Paul couldn't be listing ministry gifts in
their order of importance within the local church,
because in the passage in First Corinthians 12:28, Paul
lists teachers third. However, in Ephesians 4:11 he lists
the office of the teacher last. That's not consistent.

Also, assuming that "governments" is the pastoral
office, in First Corinthians 12:28 Paul lists the ministry
of helps before the pastoral office. If he were listing
them by their importance in the local church today,
then the teacher and the helps ministry would have
authority over the pastor in the local assembly!

That's not scriptural. And according to the list in
Ephesians 4:11, that means the evangelist would be in
authority over the pastor in the local body! That isn't biblical, particularly because the evangelist's ministry is
usually not a stationary ministry *in* the local church; it is

usually more of a roving ministry to the unsaved *outside* of the church.

So we can readily see that Paul does not list the ministry gifts in their order of importance in the local church today. Neither was he establishing the hierarchy for local church government by the order in which the ministry gifts were listed.

No, the office of the apostle was *not* listed first because it is the most important office in the local body and is supposed to rule over all the other ministry gifts. Actually, in Ephesians 4:11 and First Corinthians 12:28, it would seem logical that Paul listed these offices in that order by the way God "set" or *developed* the ministry gifts in the Early Church.

The Early Church didn't have the *fivefold* ministry to begin with because it takes time for God to develop ministries and ministers. And God doesn't put novices in positions of authority or in ministry offices because He won't violate His own Word (1 Tim. 3:6). So for a time, the apostolic ministry was the only ministry in operation in the Early Church.

Therefore, the apostolic office was the first ministry gift that was initially evident in the Early Church. The twelve Apostles of the Lamb were the only ministers in the beginning days of the Early Church. These men had companied with Jesus in His earthly ministry (Acts 1:21). They were chosen by God, and the Holy Spirit had equipped and qualified them as ministers of the gospel.

The apostles seemed to have the ability to operate in all the ministry gifts to some degree. And, really, they needed that ability because the Church was in its infancy stages and no other ministry gift had developed in the Church yet. It would also be safe to say that they ministered prophetically to some degree, and they did minister evangelistically as well. There was also an element of pastoral oversight, and we know for certain that they taught the Word.

Apostles, however, did not remain as the *only* ministry gift in the Church. As time progressed, those who ministered as prophets also began to appear. The prophets spoke by inspired utterance. The scriptures don't give us much detail on this subject, but we do know that the ministry of the prophet was well established by the time the account in Acts 13:1 occurred: *"Now there were in the church that was at Antioch certain PROPHETS. . . ."*

Similarly, the Scriptures don't give us the exact beginning of the evangelist's ministry. However, we see the office of the evangelist first mentioned in Acts 8 in Philip's ministry. By then the Church had already been in existence for many years, and there had been time for the Holy Spirit to develop the ministry of the evangelist in the Church.

Pastors or shepherds were raised up as the Church grew and believers matured spiritually (Acts 14:23; 15:2; 20:28). And the ministry of the teacher was developed in the Early Church as believers were trained and instructed in doctrine (Acts 2:42; 13:1).

Another reason it is erroneous to exalt the apostle's office above all others is that even in the Early Church, the apostles didn't govern all the churches — even churches they had helped to establish.

Paul only had *spiritual oversight* of churches while he was establishing them. But he had no oversight in the church at Jerusalem or any other church whatsoever. Once he left a church he had established, he delegated oversight to others (Acts 20:28).

After leaving, Paul did respond to questions the Church asked, and he offered godly input to them. But he did not control or govern them.

I don't really like to use the words "spiritual authority," in reference to the apostolic office because that gives the idea that apostles rule and govern people and churches, and they don't.

But the point is that in First Corinthians 12:28 when Paul said, ". . . *God hath SET some in the church* . . . ," he was probably referring to the order in which God "set" or *developed* ministry gifts in the Early Church.

Another error in this doctrine is a teaching which says that all the ministry gifts make up the "government" of the local church, and each church, regardless of its size, is to be ruled by the fivefold ministry.

Again, people haven't rightly divided the Word. They haven't distinguished between the *Church as a whole* — the universal Body of Christ — and *the local church*. In the Church as a whole, we will find all five ministry gifts in operation. But every local church will *not* have all five ministry gifts operating in its assembly.

These misconceptions really put the Body of Christ into bondage instead of liberating believers. The Bible says that the Word of God will set us free (John 8:32), not bring us into bondage.

You see, if we aren't careful, we can have misconceptions on both sides of this issue. We can get in the ditch on one side and deny the true office and function of the apostle. Or we can get in a ditch on the other side and give the apostolic office unlimited preeminence and authority.

Those who give the apostolic office too much preeminence and claim to stand in that office, seem to take the attitude, "I'm an apostle! You've got to do what I say because in order to have correct New Testament government, the local church has to be governed by apostles."

Actually, I can't find anywhere in the New Testament that there is any higher office in the local church than the pastoral office. I don't see anywhere in the New Testament where apostles ruled over pastors and other ministry gifts.

These unscriptural teachings that apostles and prophets are to rule and govern people and churches are not new. I've been in the ministry more than fifty-seven years, and I've seen these same unscriptural teachings in the Body of Christ before. These errors run in cycles. They crop up in every generation in the Church and have to be dealt with.

You see, another generation will come up that hasn't been taught the truth of God's Word on a particular subject, and they'll get off in a ditch in an area and get off-balance scripturally.

In every generation God has to raise up someone in church leadership to deal with these issues. God raised up Donald Gee in the 1930s to deal with this same extreme teaching on apostles in his book, *The Ministry-Gifts of Christ,* which is now out of print. Donald Gee was one of the pioneers and great teachers of the Pentecostal Movement.

Then we had the same problem surface again in the Body of Christ in the 1950s. Gordon Lindsay addressed it again in his book, *Apostles, Prophets and Governments,* and the problem died down. Lindsay was the founder of the Bible school, Christ For The Nations, and he published the magazine, *The Voice of Healing.* Almost all the leading healing evangelists of the day published their articles in this magazine.

Because Donald Gee and Gordon Lindsay were respected leaders in the Church, and their books were scripturally balanced, they stopped much of the wrong doctrine that had surfaced back then.

There was a real revival in those days, and that's usually when the devil starts all of these spiritual tangents to try to stop the move of God. He diverts believers by getting them off in spiritual error, trying to abort the real move of God's Spirit.

In our day, a new generation has grown up in the Church. And this same controversy has resurfaced in the Body of Christ, so it has to be addressed again. I tried to get God to have someone else do it, but He said, "No, you do it." That's the reason for this book.

I will quote from Gordon Lindsay's book, *Apostles, Prophets and Governments* from time to time in this book, because it amplifies what I believe and his insights help explain some of the things the Lord said to me in that visitation.

But one reason these errors have occurred again in our day is that people try to give the apostolic office of today the same status as the second or third class of apostle in the days of the Early Church. But it simply does not have the same status.

Now there is no doubt at all that some folks in our day could rightly be called apostles in the fourth class. (We will discuss the fourth class of apostle in the next chapter.) But a fellow who goes around broadcasting to everyone that he is an apostle, probably isn't one.

If you are a minister, I would encourage you to let others call you what they will based on the spiritual endowments or equipment and fruit they see manifested in your life and ministry. Let's just rejoice to see the ministry gifts in manifestation and glory in the work the Lord is doing in the Body of Christ without being concerned about titles.

Chapter 2
Fourth Class of Apostle: Non-Foundational Apostles

Although there are no apostles and prophets of the second or third rank in the Body of Christ today, there *is* a fourth class of apostle. There are those in the Church today who stand in the apostolic office in a measure. They are *sent ones*, but they are in a lesser class than those in the Early Church. They are in this fourth class of apostles.

Evidently the word "apostle" was more widely used in the days of the Early Church than it is now, and people understood its meaning. But since it is a word we don't use much today, people have misunderstood it. Even words today sometimes are used generally and at other times are used specifically.

You see, we can miss certain truths the Bible is trying to get across to us when we build spiritual air castles about some of these things, including misconceptions and unfounded ideas about the apostolic office. Then the Lord has to come along and knock down our air castles and correct us, and some people get mad about it.

For instance, let me point out something to you. The Greek word "apostle" is translated from the word "apostolos" meaning *a sent one*. In Philippians 2:25, Paul talks about Epaphroditus as the Philippians' messenger. The Greek word used here translated as *messenger* is the word "apostolos."

PHILIPPIANS 2:25
25 Yet I supposed it necessary to send to you Epa-
phroditus, my brother, and companion in labour,
and fellowsoldier, but your MESSENGER, and he
that ministered to my wants.

By using the word "messenger," Paul was calling
Epaphroditus an *apostle*. But Epaphroditus probably
didn't stand in the office of the apostle in the specific
sense we think of it today. As the word "apostle" is used
here, it means one *sent out* as a *delegate* or *representative* or as the *commissioned representative of a congregation*.[1]

Of course, Epaphroditus was not an apostle on the
same rank or level as Paul. He was not an apostle of
the second or third rank even though he was in the
Early Church because he did not lay New Testament
doctrine or foundation. Any apostolic ministry Epaphroditus may have fulfilled would have been in the
fourth class.

As Paul used the word "apostle" here, he probably
used it in the general sense, meaning that the church
sent Epaphroditus, much as you would send a delegate
to a convention or a meeting. Epaphroditus was an
apostle, *messenger*, or *delegate* sent from the Philippians, perhaps to simply assist Paul in the ministry.

As a messenger or delegate, it does not appear that
Epaphroditus occupied the full sphere of the apostolic
office as Paul did. Paul was not only a *messenger*, but
he also had the spiritual anointing or *ability to start
churches*.

Paul also had the *spiritual ability and equipment*

enabling him *to be responsible for the oversight* of those churches until the pastoral office could be filled in that local church. We have no record that Epaphroditus started any churches; therefore, he had no specific apostolic ministry toward any churches.

Actually, the word "apostle" was also used even in *secular* Greek writing. In other words, people who didn't even know God were called apostles. In the classical Greek, the word "apostle" used as a noun meant *a commissioned messenger* or *an ambassador.* Used as a verb it means to *send off* or *out.* A person who was sent to do a specific job was called an apostle because he was sent specifically to accomplish a certain task.

Therefore, there may be those in the Body of Christ today who stand in the apostolic office in a measure as those *sent out with a message.* They are commissioned by the Holy Spirit to bring a specific message or ministry along a certain scriptural line to the Body of Christ. They are in the fourth class of apostle.

But bear in mind that all those who stand in the office of apostle regardless of rank or class are first of all preachers or teachers of the Word, just like everyone who is called to the ministry. Or they may be both a preacher *and* a teacher. But then they also have a special call on them to fulfill a special job or bring a certain message to the Body of Christ.

Modern-Day Missionaries

Many of our modern-day missionaries are in the fourth class of apostles if they are *sent out* by the Holy

Ghost. Those sent out by missionary boards may be doing the work of a missionary, but that doesn't necessarily qualify them spiritually as an apostle.

In other words, the word "apostle" in this class implies one who is *sent out* or *commissioned* by the *Holy Spirit*, not merely one who *goes.*

Actually, a true missionary is a *sent one* by the Holy Ghost with a *message* to people in certain countries. Marvelous things happen in those countries as a result of some of these ministries.

Some missionaries not only go to a country with a message, but they have the ability to establish churches too. Those today who are really called and sent by God to establish new works in other countries are apostles, because one of the main characteristics of an apostle's ministry is that he establishes churches and pioneers new works.

For example, Paul established many of the Gentile churches we read about in the Book of Acts. Missionaries today are doing the work of the apostle if they not only have the ability to get people saved as the evangelist does, but they also have the ability to start and establish churches.

Then once people are saved, an apostle also has the God-given ability and the spiritual qualities to pastor, nurture, teach, and establish people in the Word. He stays with the work long enough to get it established and then may go on to pioneer other new works.

Over the years, I've seen folks who went from city to city and established good churches everywhere they went. That was their call, and it is part of the apostle's office. The ministry of the apostle has been in the Body of Christ all the time, but we've just called them missionaries or church planters. Really, the *title* is not the main issue; the *function* is.

In the early days of the Pentecostal Movement, I remember one particular fellow who could rightly be called an apostle. In a short period of time he established fifty churches in the country where God sent him. No doubt he was an apostle to that country.

Years ago I heard a Full Gospel preacher say that he had spent seven years in a certain country where he had tried to establish a church. After seven years, the most he ever had in his congregation was thirty-seven people, and thirty-five of those were children he had picked up off the streets. He got so discouraged, he came back to America, deciding never to return to the mission field.

But he got to praying, and God got ahold of him. God showed him where his problem was. He hadn't known his rights and privileges in Christ and how to appropriate the promises in God's Word. When he began to understand his inheritance in Christ and how to believe God, God sent him back to that country. After a period of time, he came back to preach in America, and that's when I heard him.

He said, "In this past year, we've had 270,000 people saved, 70,000 filled with the Holy Spirit, and in one year's time, we have built 80 churches." That was in *one* year! His fruitful ministry along this line indicated the apostolic call on his life. You see, he fulfilled the *function* of the apostle; he wasn't necessarily concerned about the title "apostle."

Pastors Who Stand in the Apostolic Office

As I said, the word "apostle" seems to have a much broader sense than we have given it. I think that's one reason we have gotten into error in this area; we haven't understood the full scope of the office. An apostle in the fourth class can be a *messenger*, a representative, an *ambassador* of the gospel, a *missionary*, or one who is *sent out* on a special *mission* with a special *message*.

Sometimes in our day we seem to have the idea that there are very few apostles, when many of them have been standing in that office all the time. We just haven't called them that.

For example, a pastor can sometimes stand in the apostolic office in a measure in this fourth class if he is *sent* by the Holy Ghost to build a church in a certain city. In that sense, he is a *sent one* to that city or community with a *message*.

Of course, not every pastor sent to a city would qualify as an apostle. He would also have to possess the other characteristics and spiritual qualities of the apostolic call operating in his life and ministry, which we'll cover later.

Even so, a true pastor called to start a work for God wouldn't advertise himself as an apostle. He wouldn't be concerned with labels. His motives would not be to lift himself up, but to complete what God has sent him to do.

In Acts 1:20, we see some indication that a pastor can stand in a measure in the office of the apostle. You remember that Judas had fallen through transgression, and another had to be chosen to take his place.

> **ACTS 1:20**
> **20 For it is written in the book of Psalms, Let his [Judas'] habitation be desolate, and let no man dwell therein: and his BISHOPRICK let another take.**

The word "bishoprick" indicates the office of the *bishop*. In First Timothy 3:1,2, Paul calls *pastors* "bishops."

> **1 TIMOTHY 3:1,2**
> **1   This is a true saying, If a man desire the office of a BISHOP** [pastor or overseer], **he desireth a good work.**
> **2   A BISHOP** [pastor or overseer] **then must be blameless, the husband of one wife, vigilant, sober, of good behaviour, given to hospitality, apt to teach.**

The word "bishop" is the Greek work "episkopos," which is translated *bishop* or *overseer*. The overseer of the local church is the *pastor* (Acts 20:28).

A pastor may build one church, and he may even be sent to a particular city or group of people with a message. In that sense he is standing in the office of the apostle in a measure because he is a sent one by the Holy Ghost with a message. His message is always the gospel.

Then you can see how absurd it is when some young upstart comes to a pastor who is standing in that apostolic office even in a measure, and says, "You don't have the right church government. You don't have an apostle in authority over you."

In the first place, that's not scriptural. A pastor doesn't need an apostle over him. In the second place, he may well be an apostle himself in a limited measure! Now a pastor might not be an apostle to the Church at large. But if God sent him, he could be an apostle, a sent one, to that city and to that local church.

However, as a sent one, that would not give the pastor authority over everyone in that city or over other churches. But his call would be accompanied by the divine ability to establish and oversee that local church.

This is a broader meaning of the word "apostle" than we have thought. And in our day, sad to say, some folks have taken advantage of the ignorance of some people to mislead them by calling themselves apostles, so they could exercise authority over others.

The Greek word that is most commonly translated "apostle" is *apostolos*. The verb is sometimes used with the same meaning: to send one on a mission as an envoy. It can mean a delegate; specifically an ambassador of the gospel.

Used as a verb the word "apostle" means *to send*. The word for "bishoprick" in Acts 1:20 referring to the Apostles of the Lamb is *overseer*. So we can see a relationship between these two words — apostle and overseer. And we can see by observation in the New Testament that there was an element of pastoral oversight in the apostolic ministry, as the apostles were getting churches established.

In the classical Greek, the word was commonly used. Greek writings talk about "apostles of Zeus," or those who were sent out to represent the gods. Biblically, apostles were sent out to represent the true God.

The Bible uses the word "apostle" to get across the

idea that there are those who are especially sent to do a work for God. They may even be overseers, which refers to the pastoral office.

Do we have an example in the Scriptures of an overseer — a pastor — standing in the office of the apostle? Yes, we do. Paul called James, the Lord's brother, an apostle. Paul said, *"But other of the APOSTLES saw I none, save JAMES the Lord's brother"* (Gal. 1:19).

James wasn't one of the original apostles. He didn't even believe Jesus was the Son of God when Jesus was here on the earth. The Bible indicates that Jesus appeared to James in a vision (1 Cor. 15:7).

But in Acts 15 we can see that when a meeting was called of the elders and apostles to determine church doctrine, James was the overseer of that Jerusalem meeting (Acts 12:17; Acts 15:13). It seems that James headed up or *pastored* the Jerusalem church, yet he was called an *apostle*.

Other Non-Foundational Apostles

Therefore, we will find the fourth class of apostolic ministry operating in a measure in the Body of Christ in the sense of "one sent forth" by the Holy Spirit to do a certain job, or to bring a certain emphasis along a biblical line of truth to the Body of Christ. It is not so important that the ministry is in *title*, but it is important that it is in *demonstration* and *power* (1 Cor. 2:4).

From time to time God sends someone to the Church with a message to stir believers up along a certain scriptural line. The person is *sent* just to do that.

So we find apostles in this fourth class who are especially called of God with certain messages and ministries to the Church at large — the Body of Christ.

For instance, there is no doubt that God called Smith Wigglesworth as a *sent one* to the Body of Christ as "an apostle of faith." Wigglesworth was raised up by the Holy Spirit for the purpose of teaching the Church about faith. In that sense, he was an apostle — *a sent one* — to the Church, and faith was his scriptural *message* to the Body of Christ.

Several years ago I visited with an Assemblies of God minister from Great Britain, and he told me that he had known Wigglesworth personally. Wigglesworth had preached his last sermon in this man's church. He told me, "I personally know of twenty-three people who were raised from the dead under Wigglesworth's ministry." This wasn't hearsay; this man personally knew of these cases.

Wigglesworth never called himself an apostle. He was wise in not doing so. Others called him an "apostle of faith." What does that mean? Did that mean Wigglesworth had authority over other ministry gifts in the Body of Christ? No. It just meant he was a sent one to bring a message to the Body of Christ and to do a certain work for God.

Wigglesworth was raised up by God to build up, edify, and benefit the Body of Christ along a particular scriptural line — teaching and demonstrating *faith*. And solid, scriptural works were started from his revivals on every inhabited continent of the earth.

In that sense we have apostles today who are sent

forth just to emphasize one particular message to the Body of Christ. These ministries are not called to exercise authority over others or lay any more foundation to the New Testament.

I saw apostolic ministries in operation when I came over among the Pentecostals, even though we didn't call them that. These were people who not only were sent out with a message, but also had the ability to start churches.

For example, there was a woman evangelist who pioneered new works throughout north and northeast Texas. Her husband got saved in one of her meetings; he was a building contractor. He had the ability to lead singing, so he quit his business and led the singing in their revival meetings and took care of the preliminaries.

This was in the '30s and '40s, and many towns back then didn't have any Full Gospel churches of any kind in that area. But even in Depression Days, this woman and her husband would go into these different towns and hold open-air meetings all summer long.

This woman would preach two or three weeks, and maybe only one or two people would attend the meetings. But she just kept on preaching, and her husband sang, and finally a few more people would start coming to the meetings.

She would preach about salvation, and people would get saved. Actually, she could get more people saved accidentally than most people could on purpose. Finally word got around, and many people would come to the meetings and get saved.

Since her husband was a contractor, they would stay in a place long enough to erect a church building and she would start a church.

But she told me, "If I stayed more than two years in any one place, the work would start to fail because I'm not called to be a pastor. So I would just stay long enough to start a church, and then I would turn it over to a pastor."

This woman started many churches, and some of those churches are still in existence today after fifty or sixty years because she established them on a solid scriptural foundation. There is no doubt in my mind that she was operating in the apostolic office in a measure, even though she was really considered to be an evangelist.

She operated in the apostolic office *in a measure.* Once she had established a church and had turned it over to a pastor, she and her husband just went on to start another church somewhere else. In other words, she was a church pioneer. Apostles are very often pioneers of new works.

Throughout my years of ministry, I've never seen anyone who has fit the qualifications of those in the second or third class of apostle. And after Jesus spoke to me in the 1987 visitation, I understood why I haven't. We won't see that class in the Body of Christ today. But I have seen those who fit the qualifications of the fourth class of apostle.

I saw others whom God called and sent to fulfill certain functions in the Body of Christ or to fulfill a special ministry along a certain scriptural line. In that sense, they were "sent ones." But they didn't go around calling themselves apostles. That's where people make a mistake. It's not necessary to give people titles; we all just need to be faithful to do what God has called us to do.

Some of these people weren't apostles in the fullest sense. But they did stand in that office in a measure because they were sent ones to bring a special message or to carry out a special ministry to the Body of Christ.

Actually, throughout church history, God has raised up people and sent them to spearhead revivals and to do other mighty works for Him. And in that sense, we could probably legitimately call them "apostles" in this lesser class.

I remember one fellow in particular in the early days of the Pentecostal Movement who seemed to have a ministry of getting people filled with the Holy Ghost. For that reason, pastors from all over the area would invite him to come to their churches. Many pastors told me, "He just seems to have the supernatural ability to get people baptized in the Holy Ghost. Everywhere he goes, people are filled with the Spirit."

In other words, he was a *messenger* to the Body of Christ teaching specifically about the baptism of the Holy Spirit. There are others who are special messengers along other scriptural lines. We need all of them in the Body of Christ.

I believe there are ministers who have been operating in a measure in some form of the apostolic office, but people have been so religiously brainwashed, they haven't recognized it. The Body of Christ needs to be aware of this scriptural office and its function, so valid

ministers can operate in the full sphere to which they
are called by God.

---

[1] Kittel, *Theological Dictionary of the New Testament* (Paternoster Press:
Eerdmans Publishing Company, 1985), p. 70.

Chapter 3
Characteristics of the Apostolic Call

The Bible gives certain general characteristics that are true for anyone who is called to the apostolic office regardless of rank or class. If a person's life and ministry does not possess these general characteristics, I would seriously doubt the true nature of the apostolic call in his life.

Called and *Separated* by God; *Confirmed* by Man

Using Paul's ministry as a biblical example of an apostle, we can see that a person needs to be *called* by *God* before his call to the apostolic ministry is ever *confirmed* by *man*. We can see the truth of this principle when Paul was separated by the Holy Ghost to the apostolic ministry in Acts chapter 13.

ACTS 13:1-4
1 Now there were in the church that was at Antioch certain PROPHETS and TEACHERS; as Barnabas, and Simeon that was called Niger, and Lucius of Cyrene, and Manaen, which had been brought up with Herod the tetrarch, and Saul [or Paul].
2 As they ministered to the Lord, and fasted, the HOLY GHOST said, SEPARATE ME Barnabas and Saul FOR THE WORK whereunto I HAVE CALLED THEM.

**3   And when they had fasted and prayed, and laid
their hands on them, they sent them away.
4   So they, being SENT FORTH by the HOLY
GHOST** [an apostle is a sent one]**, departed unto
Seleucia; and from thence they sailed to Cyprus.**

I want you to see the progression of Paul's ministry
here. These scriptures give us a list of five men. These
men were each either a prophet *or* a teacher, or a
prophet *and* a teacher. We gather from the Scriptures
that Barnabas was a teacher not a prophet, because a
prophet is one who has visions and revelations. We
have no indication from the Scriptures that Barnabas
had any visions or revelations.

On the other hand, Paul was a prophet *and* a teacher.
We know Paul was a prophet because he wrote almost
half of the New Testament, and he received it by revelation. Remember Paul said, *"How that BY REVELATION
he made known unto me the mystery . . ."* (Eph. 3:3).

So up until this time, this was the extent of Paul
and Barnabas' ministries — Barnabas was a teacher,
and Paul was a prophet *and* a teacher. And by this
time, both Paul and Barnabas had been in the ministry
for some time. But neither Paul nor Barnabas had
stepped into the apostolic office until they were separated and sent out by the Holy Ghost for the work God
had for them, which was the apostolic ministry.

We know it was the apostolic ministry Paul and
Barnabas were called to because the Bible says they
were *"sent forth"* by the Holy Ghost for the *work* He had
called them to: *"So they, being SENT FORTH by the*

Holy Ghost . . ." (Acts 13:4). Then the Scriptures go on to tell about the apostles' first missionary journey. And later on that first missionary journey, the Scriptures call both Paul and Barnabas "apostles" (Acts 14:14).

But I want you to see something in Acts 13:2. Paul and Barnabas were *called* to the apostolic ministry by God from the foundation of the world (Eph. 1:4). But in this passage of Scripture that call was *confirmed* by man by prophecy and the laying on of hands.

In other words, Paul and Barnabas didn't receive their *call* to the apostolic ministry that day *by men* when hands were laid on them. Paul and Barnabas just received the *confirmation* of the apostolic call through men by the laying on of hands and prophecy. The Holy Spirit separated them to the work God had *already* called them to.

How do we know that? Because notice the Holy Ghost didn't say, "Separate unto me Barnabas and Saul for the work whereunto I *am calling* them." No! He said, *". . . Separate me Barnabas and Saul for the work whereunto I HAVE CALLED them"* (Acts 13:2). That is past tense.

It is past tense because the Holy Spirit had already spoken to Paul and Barnabas about their call to the apostolic office. This prophetic utterance was just a confirmation of the apostolic call God had already placed on their lives.

You won't find anywhere in the New Testament where believers are called and separated to a ministry office by *people*. Sometimes God may use people to *con-*

firm the call a person already has in his own spirit, but people can't call or *set* anyone into the ministry.

Sometimes people say, "But God used me to prophesy to someone that he was going to be used in the such-and-such a ministry." God may occasionally use someone to prophesy that a person will eventually be used in a certain way by the Holy Ghost.

But no one can *give* spiritual gifts or bestow ministry gifts on people through prophecy. Some people today are trying to put people into the ministry through the laying on of hands and prophecy! That's impossible and unscriptural.

We had an outbreak of this in 1949. The people involved in this movement were scriptural in many areas, but there was some error in their doctrine.

Many times ninety percent of what a person teaches can be scriptural. But ten percent can be poisonous, and it can still be very damaging to you spiritually. That's why you need to have enough Bible sense to rightly divide the Word of truth.

You need to divide or learn to separate the ninety percent that is scriptural from the ten percent that is unscriptural. And sometimes it would be more beneficial not to fellowship with those who are teaching wrong doctrine because the error could eventually harm you.

In this teaching that became popular in the '40s, so-called apostles and prophets were supposedly imparting ministry gifts and spiritual gifts through the laying on of hands and prophecy, and "putting" people into ministry offices. That is unscriptural.

Although it *is* scriptural to lay hands on people for healing or to be filled with the Holy Spirit, you can't give someone a spiritual gift or call someone into the ministry by laying hands on them. As I said, sometimes God will *confirm* a person's call through prophecy; but only God can *call* someone to the ministry or *impart* a spiritual gift to them.

Then we had another outbreak of this error in the beginning of the Charismatic Movement. And again today we are experiencing another outbreak of it.

Some of the ministers who have recently gotten off into error in this area weren't there years ago when these errors surfaced earlier in the Body of Christ. Therefore, they didn't know the harm this teaching caused in the past.

That's why if they had good sense, younger ministers would listen to some of us who have been over the road spiritually before them. It would save them many heartaches. Some of them could lose their churches over these false doctrines. And some of them will ultimately be embarrassed because these teachings are unscriptural and will eventually be shown to be wrong.

First a Preacher or Teacher

Another general characteristic of the apostolic call is that an apostle is first and foremost a preacher *or* a teacher, or a preacher *and* a teacher of the Word.

1 TIMOTHY 2:7
7   Whereunto I am ORDAINED a PREACHER,

> **and an APOSTLE, (I speak the truth in Christ, and
> lie not;) a TEACHER OF THE GENTILES in faith
> and verity.**
>
> **2 TIMOTHY 1:11**
> **11 Whereunto I am APPOINTED a PREACHER,
> and an APOSTLE, and a TEACHER of THE GEN-
> TILES.**

Notice Paul didn't say, "I am first ordained an
apostle." No, Paul said first, "I am ordained a *preacher,*"
because he was first and foremost a *preacher* of the
good news. He was a *sent one* for the purpose of preaching and teaching the *gospel.*

Every single one of the ministry gifts is first of all a
preacher or a teacher of the Word. In other words, those
called to ministry gifts either *proclaim* or *explain* the
Bible.

We can see by this passage that an apostle's *main*
ministry is to preach or teach the Word. The apostolic
call has nothing to do with ruling over churches or
people. In both of these scriptures, Paul mentions his
preaching ministry first to emphasize the apostle's primary ministry.

Paul was a preacher of what? The *gospel.* A teacher
of what? God's *Word.* That should help us understand
the true nature of the apostolic call when some of these
fellows come around teaching doctrine other than the
Word, calling themselves apostles.

Signs of a True Apostle

The signs of an apostle are stated by Paul in Second

Corinthians 12.

> **2 CORINTHIANS 12:12**
> **12 Truly the SIGNS OF AN APOSTLE were wrought among you in all patience, in SIGNS, and WONDERS, and MIGHTY DEEDS.**

What are the signs of an apostle? *Signs, wonders,* and *mighty deeds.* If some of these folks who call themselves apostles today don't have some of these same apostolic signs working in their lives and ministries, then they are not in that office.

Also, to stand in this office, one must have a very deep, personal experience with the Lord — something very real and beyond the ordinary.

Paul, for example, had such an experience with the Lord in his conversion experience and evidently throughout his ministry. Although Paul did not see Jesus in the flesh when Jesus walked upon the earth, Paul saw Jesus in a vision (Acts 9:3-6). His conversion was beyond the ordinary and deeply spiritual (Acts 26:13-19).

For example, Paul had such a deep spiritual experience with the Lord that Paul received his knowledge of the Lord's Supper — a New Testament church sacrament — directly from Jesus: *"For I have received of the Lord that which also I delivered unto you . . ."* (1 Cor. 11:23).

As a foundational apostle and prophet, Paul received insight and instruction concerning this church ordinance directly from the Lord — not from the other apostles, nor from church tradition. And, of course, Paul received the revelation of the gospel from the Lord (Gal. 2:1,2).

Those in the fourth class of apostle won't receive any more foundational revelation upon which the Church will be established. But their personal experience with the Lord will be supernatural and beyond the ordinary. However, that does not make an apostle personally superior to other believers or other ministry gifts.

If these are the signs of a *true* apostle, what are the signs of a *false* apostle?

False Apostles

If there were false apostles and prophets in the Early Church, we are not so perfected in our day that we won't have them in the Church today. But that doesn't do away with the genuine office of the apostle. In fact, if anything, it proves there is a genuine apostolic office because Satan only counterfeits what is real and genuine.

> **2 CORINTHIANS 11:13-15**
> **13 For such are FALSE APOSTLES, DECEITFUL WORKERS, transforming themselves into the apostles of Christ.**
> **14 And no marvel; for Satan himself is transformed into an angel of light.**
> **15 Therefore it is no great thing if his ministers also be transformed as the ministers of righteousness; whose end shall be ACCORDING TO THEIR WORKS.**

There is one very simple way to distinguish a false apostle from a true apostle. A true apostle *plants* and *establishes* new works in the Lord on a sound biblical foundation — the Word of God.

A false apostle *tears up* works with division, strife, and wrong teaching. Some so-called apostles today are doing that, and they are *false* apostles.

> **PHILIPPIANS 1:15-17**
> **15 Some indeed preach Christ even of ENVY and STRIFE; and some also of good will:**
> **16 The one preach Christ of CONTENTION, NOT SINCERELY** [not honestly]**, supposing to add afflic-tion to my bonds:**
> **17 But the other of love, knowing that I am set for the defence of the gospel.**

Did you ever see a counterfeit three-dollar bill? Of course not. That's because there isn't any such thing as a three-dollar bill. A false apostle is a counterfeit of a genuine apostle and tries to act like the real thing.

The Bible says a false apostle is a deceitful worker. He usually counterfeits the genuine office out of impure motives for reasons of personal gain.

That is one reason I ask these folks who claim to be apostles, "How many churches have you pioneered?" Or "What are your qualifications which prove you stand in that office?"

They may have started one church. But pioneering just one work doesn't necessarily qualify them as an apostle because there are other characteristics and spir-itual qualities that go along with the apostolic office as well. And they may not possess those characteristics and qualities. It may be that pioneering and pastoring that one work is the main ministry the Lord has for them.

Gordon Lindsay in his book, *Apostles, Prophets and Governments,* had something to say about false apostles:

> A false apostle is identified first by his usurping of the office of an apostle, and second, by failing to produce the works of an apostle. The Early Church took note of those who claimed apostleship but in fact were false apostles. They were tried and found liars and exposed so that they would not be able to lead away the sheep of the Church of Christ.
>
> It is evident that the office of an apostle is needed in the church today. But history shows the danger of any man calling himself an apostle. Groups that have attempted to restore apostolic functions by electing apostles have merely exposed their own folly. Those claiming to be apostles sometimes have at the beginning manifested a generous spirit. But they soon became arbitrary and sectarian. And usually succeeded in bringing people under bondage.[1]

A pastor went to a certain place and heard a fellow preaching who claimed to be an apostle. You certainly couldn't see any *works* or *fruit* of the apostolic office in the fellow's ministry. He hadn't established any churches, nor did he possess any of the other characteristics of the apostolic office.

But as soon as this so-called apostle convinced others he was an "apostle," he announced, "To get the proper New Testament church government, an apostle and prophet need to be in authority over the pastor in the local assembly. I'm an apostle. The churches in this area are to come under my authority. All of you are to send at least twenty percent of your income to me."

This so-called apostle was trying to use his "authority" in order to bring people under bondage and to extort money from them! I would call him a false apostle. His motives were wrong and so were his methods.

But one of the pastors who heard him say this, swallowed this erroneous teaching hook, line, and sinker and submitted his church to this so-called apostle's "authority." The pastor had a two-hundred-member congregation. But after he submitted his ministry to this so-called apostle, the pastor's congregation dwindled to fifty people before he realized this wasn't scriptural.

The people in his congregation had more sense than the pastor did. They left the church because they knew this teaching wasn't correct.

Then this so-called apostle said, "Any church that doesn't have an apostle over it is an illegitimate church."

I'd just as soon hear a donkey bray at midnight in a tin barn! Actually, I'd have more respect for the donkey because braying is all he *can* do.

You see, the work of a true apostle will include not only the fruit of the spirit, but it will also be displayed by his concern for the upbuilding of the Body of Christ — not tearing it down with unscriptural teachings.

Gordon Lindsay talks about the work of true apostles in his book, *Apostles, Prophets and Governments:*

True apostles will first manifest their apostolic ministry by humility. They will reveal the ministry that God has given them by their works rather than by public proclamation of their office. One can do the work of an apostle without calling himself an apostle. The office of an apostle is to a great extent misunderstood. Many think it is an elevation to a position of authority whereby one may rule over God's people. . . . Let one do the works of an apostle and he will find that his ministry will become recognized. . . .

An apostle will have a burden for the whole Church, and he will be interested in the welfare of the entire Church. That does not mean that he will physically minister to all members of the Body, which may number millions. But his burden will be for the whole Church of Christ. . . .

A true apostle will manifest an interest in the whole body and will labor to the edifying to the whole body until all members "come into the unity of the faith."

He will not have a covetous spirit or be a seeker after financial gain.[2]

Brother Lindsay wrote this in the '50s, but you would think he was writing it for us today, wouldn't you?

A Submitted Ministry

I want you to see something else about the biblical characteristics of a true apostle.

> **GALATIANS 2:1,2**
> **1　Then fourteen years after I went up again to Jerusalem with Barnabas, and took Titus with me also.**
> **2　And I went up by revelation, and COMMUNI-CATED UNTO THEM that gospel which I PREACH AMONG THE GENTILES, but privately to them which were of reputation, lest by any means I should run, or had run, in vain.**

There are several things to note in this passage. An

apostle is not above other ministry gifts. In fact, a true apostle will submit his ministry to other proven ministers of the gospel, as Paul did here.

No one knows how long Paul was in Arabia (Gal. 1:17), but we do know that Paul had been in the ministry at least seventeen years (Gal. 1:18; 2:1) when he went up to Jerusalem to confer with the apostles there. In other words, he was not a novice in ministry, yet he still conferred with other men of reputation about what he preached.

In fact it was revealed to Paul by the Holy Spirit that he should go to Jerusalem and share the gospel he was preaching to the Gentiles to "those of reputation" — the outstanding chief apostles at Jerusalem. The apostles at Jerusalem did not preach to the Gentiles; they were still preaching to the Jews.

Paul said he submitted the revelation God gave him to the apostles, ". . . *lest by any means I should run, or had run, in vain*" (Gal. 2:2). In other words, Paul submitted his revelation of the gospel of the Lord Jesus Christ to the spiritual leaders of his day.

If there is a possibility that this great man of God could run in vain, there is a possibility that we could run in vain too. That's why Paul wanted to submit his revelation to the Apostles of the Lamb. They were proven and well-established ministers of the gospel and had companied with Jesus in His earth walk.

If Paul needed to submit his revelation to proven ministers, how much more should we? Yet some folks in our day want to confer with those who have recently

become leaders in the ministry or who are young in
ministry, or they don't want to submit their revelations
or ministries to anyone at all.

A minister came to me once with his great "revelation." I told him, "I can't accept that because it is not
scriptural." I knew it would hurt the Body of Christ,
hinder the plan of God, and eventually shipwreck this
man's ministry.

"Yes, but God gave me *my* revelation," he insisted.

You're in trouble the minute you go talking like
that. If God has shown you something, others in the
Church will know it, too, especially those who are leaders in the Church. But beware of any revelation that
lifts you up in pride and exalts you instead of exalting
the Lord Jesus Christ.

I told this minister, "Even with the office of the
prophet, Paul said, *'Let the prophets speak two or three,
and let the other judge'* (1 Cor. 14:29). If the prophet's
ministry is to be judged, then the teacher's ministry or
any other ministry would also need to be judged. You
don't judge the person; you judge what he's teaching or
preaching. You judge the person's *ministry*."

But this man wouldn't listen and went out and
started teaching his so-called revelation to the Body of
Christ. But his ministry didn't last because his teaching
wasn't scriptural; it was all *"me"* and *"mine."* He got
lifted up in pride and concocted a revelation that wasn't
biblical. He eventually faded off the scene and no one
ever heard of him again.

If you have a revelation about the Word, prove it out

scripturally first before you teach or preach it publicly. Then submit it to others of established reputation in the Body of Christ, and let them judge it. Don't preach it or act on it until men of reputation who are seasoned in ministry have judged it. You don't want to run in vain.

Actually, we ought to want our revelations and our ministries to be judged. Paul wanted his revelation and ministry to be judged. He wanted it to be right and scripturally sound. That's why he submitted it to the apostles at Jerusalem who were well seasoned in ministry.

The fruit of a true apostle is that he has a submitted attitude toward other brethren, including the pastors of local bodies where he might minister on occasion. He is concerned about blessing and building up and establishing works, not tearing them down with questionable teachings and revelations.

In my ministry, I've also practiced submitting revelations I've received from the Lord to those of reputation. And when I was in the field ministry, although I was not an apostle, I did what any traveling ministry, including an apostle, should do. First, I always submitted my ministry to the pastor or overseer of the local church where I ministered.

I've always told the pastor of local churches where I ministered, "If there is anything I'm preaching that you don't want me to preach, just tell me and I won't preach on it. If there is anything I'm not preaching on and you want me to preach on it, just tell me."

That is true submission, and every traveling teacher should submit his ministry to the pastor of a local body.

Most of the time, the pastor would tell me to take my liberty and minister however God was leading me. But, you see, I had proven my ministry and had gained the pastor's trust.

I've practiced that when it comes to revelations I've received from the Word too. I've always submitted major revelations I've received from the Holy Spirit to brethren I knew and had confidence in who were well respected in the ministry, just as Paul did in Galatians 2:2.

These men of God weren't novices, nor fellows who were fly-by-nights. They were ministers who were spiritually sound and had held steady in ministry for years.

In Paul's ministry, we can see the general characteristics of the apostolic call. Although he was a member of a local body, he was *sent out* by the Holy Ghost. He was first and foremost a *preacher* just like every other minister. And his *message* was the gospel of the Lord Jesus Christ.

He was *commissioned* by God to bring that message to a specific group of people — the Gentiles. His apostolic ministry didn't extend to everyone. He did not have unlimited apostolic authority. Paul also had the *fruit* of a biblical apostolic ministry. And he *submitted his ministry* to those of proven reputation in the Word.

---

[1] Gordon Lindsay, *Apostles, Prophets and Governments*, (Dallas, Texas: Christ For The Nations, Inc., reprint 1988), pp. 12,13.
[2] Lindsay, p. 14.

Chapter 4
Qualifications for the Apostolic Ministry

What do the Scriptures say about the qualifications of those called to the apostolic office? First Timothy chapter 3 talks about the qualifications of a bishop or overseer, which I feel refers to the pastoral office.

We don't have any qualifications given to us specifically for the office of the apostle, prophet, evangelist, or teacher. But God would not require more of one ministry gift than He would of the others because He is no respecter of persons (Acts 10:34).

Therefore, we could safely say that the qualifications listed in First Timothy 3:1-13 are the qualifications for the ministry and apply to any ministry gift in the Body of Christ, including the apostolic office.

1 TIMOTHY 3:1-7
1 This is a true saying, If a man desire the office of a BISHOP [overseer or pastor], he desireth a good work.
2 A BISHOP then MUST BE BLAMELESS, the husband of one wife, vigilant, sober, of good behaviour, given to hospitality, APT TO TEACH;
3 Not given to wine, no striker, NOT GREEDY OF FILTHY LUCRE; but patient, not a brawler, not covetous;
4 One that ruleth well his own house, having his children in subjection with all gravity;
5 (For if a man know not how to rule his own house, how shall he take care of the church of God?)

57

**6   NOT A NOVICE, lest being lifted up with pride
he fall into the condemnation of the devil.
7   Moreover HE MUST HAVE A GOOD REPORT
of them which are without; lest he fall into
reproach and the snare of the devil.**

I've said that one who stands in the apostle's office
must have the *call* of God upon him and the spiritual
equipment enabling him to stand in that office. Both of
these elements are *God's* responsibility.

However, one called to the apostolic office must also
have the *qualifications* to stand in that office. That is
the *minister's* responsibility. Only he can qualify himself to be able to stand in such an office of trust and
responsibility.

I have seen men who were *called* of God, *equipped*
with the supernatural ability to stand in a ministry
office, but they failed in the ministry because they
lacked the *qualifications* necessary to stand in such a
ministry. They didn't prepare themselves to stand in
the ministry God had called them to.

Character and Conduct

What are some of the qualifications of a minister
called to the apostolic office or to any ministry for that
matter? First Timothy 3:2 says he must be "blameless."

I'm going to quote from other translations of this
same verse to help you see this qualification more clearly.

**1 TIMOTHY 3:2 (*Twentieth Century*)
2   ... a man of blameless character. ...**

1 TIMOTHY 3:2 (*Weymouth*)
2 . . . a man of irreproachable character. . . .

1 TIMOTHY 3:2 (*Amplified*)
2 . . . must give no grounds for accusation but must be above reproach. . . .

1 TIMOTHY 3:2 (*Taylor*)
2 . . . must be a good man whose life cannot be spoken against.

First Timothy 3:2 says, "*. . . vigilant, sober, of good behaviour. . . .*"

The Twentieth Century New Testament says, "He should live a sober, discreet, and well-ordered life."

The *Weymouth* translation says, "A minister then must be a man of irreproachable character, true to his one wife, temperate, sober-minded, well-behaved. . . ."

The Amplified Bible says he must be "circumspect and temperate and self-controlled; [he must be] sensible and well behaved and dignified and lead an orderly (disciplined) life. . . ."

I didn't think up those qualifications for the ministry. The Holy Spirit inspired Paul to write that. You see, entering the ministry is a grave responsibility. That's why every minister, including an apostle, must be dignified and lead an orderly, disciplined life. That statement alone leaves out some ministers!

In other words, a minister's life must reflect the call of God, not only in spiritual equipment, but in conduct and character. His character must be worthy of his call.

An apostle or a minister must be irreproachable in his conduct and habits. If ministers don't measure up to the qualifications, they will never reach their full potential in ministry. Some ministers are going to have to make the necessary adjustments in order to fulfill the ministry the Lord has for them.

Some ministers may sense a call to an apostolic type of ministry. As they are faithful in serving God in their current position and take time waiting in God's Presence in prayer and in the Word, a time will come when there will be a quickening of His Spirit in their spirit. Then they will be able to walk in the ability of God to fulfill their call.

Their purpose won't be to attract people to follow them, but to call upon men and women to follow Jesus. A true apostle with the character of Christ humbles himself before the Lord and endeavors never to attract attention unto himself.

Jesus said, *". . . if I be lifted up from the earth,* [I] *will draw all men unto me"* (John 12:32). One called to the apostolic office who has taken the time to develop his character would rather hide himself and lift up Jesus.

We all need to examine ourselves and get to work on developing our character and conduct to make sure it reflects the high calling of Christ. If believers need to examine themselves, how much more do those who are called of God to the apostolic office need to lay aside every weight that would try to hinder them from their high calling in Christ.

Apt To Teach Sound Doctrine

1 TIMOTHY 3:2
**2   A bishop then must be blameless . . . vigilant,
sober, of good behaviour, given to hospitality, APT
TO TEACH.**

A true apostle will also qualify himself by being apt
to teach sound biblical doctrine, not doctrinal tangents
or extreme teachings. And he will make sure he bases
his ministry solidly on the Word, rather than on spiritual gifts or signs and wonders.

Folks miss it when they think they can follow the
doctrine of some so-called apostle because they see
miraculous signs and wonders operating in his ministry.
No, every minister's doctrine must line up with the
Bible, even if signs and wonders occur in his ministry.

Rev. P. C. Nelson was a leading Greek and Hebrew
scholar and an outstanding Bible teacher. He said
something along this line about John Alexander Dowie
that has helped me immeasurably over the years.

Dowie was a great pioneer in the message of divine
healing in America. Many wonderful miracles of healing took place under Dowie's ministry. However, Dowie
got off doctrinally by announcing that he was the third
Elijah that was to come. Dad Nelson, as we called him,
said about Dowie: "You can follow Dowie's *faith*, but you
can't follow his *doctrine*."

Friends, go back to the Old Testament and read the
story of Samson. You can see in Samson's life that signs
and wonders operated in his life, but that didn't neces-

sarily mean he had godly character *or* sound doctrine.

For example, Samson had the working of miracles operating through him. Even when he was living with a woman in adultery and lying, the gift of working of miracles still operated in his life for a time (*see* Judges chapter 16). Now don't misunderstand me. The time came when God judged Samson's sin. Samson got up and shook himself and he *". . . wist not that the LORD was departed from him"* (Judges 16:20).

Well, thank God for the miracles that operated in Samson's life, but his life wasn't a moral standard to follow after.

Innocent people are misled when they try to follow someone's doctrine because of supernatural signs and wonders occurring in his ministry. Paul said, *"Be ye followers of me, EVEN AS I ALSO AM OF CHRIST"* (1 Cor. 11:1).

You can follow a person in doctrine as he follows the *Word*. But don't pay any attention to any so-called apostle or any minister if what he says can't be backed up with the Word.

Just because a person stands in a ministry office doesn't mean you ought to listen to what he says if it's not scriptural — even if the miraculous power of God is demonstrated in his life for a time. The time is coming when God will have to judge doctrinal error.

You may be able to follow someone's faith, but not his doctrine. Sometimes people try to follow someone's doctrine *because of* his faith. But that's not scriptural.

A little doctrinal error left unchecked will eventually become gross error. For example, if you flew from Tulsa to Los Angeles and you were a little bit off course, if the pilot didn't correct the course, you'd get so far off course, you'd never reach your destination.

The same thing is true spiritually. If you get off course spiritually just a little, you need to correct yourself immediately and get right back in line with the Word. Otherwise, the further you go, the greater the doctrinal error will be.

A true apostle will teach sound biblical doctrine. And he will back up what he says with the Word.

Not a Lover of Money

The Bible gives one of the qualifications for those in the ministry as a person ". . . *not greedy of filthy lucre . . .*" (1 Tim. 3:3). The Bible has much to say about ministers of the gospel and how they obtain money. In *The Worrell New Testament*, the footnote for First Timothy 3:2 says the minister of the gospel must not use "his office to extort money from people."

Over the years, I have sometimes seen people use their ministries and the anointing that is upon them to obtain money from people. For example, I once visited a certain minister's meetings, who had a marvelous healing ministry. In this particular meeting, five deaf and mute people were brought from the state institution to be healed. This man ministered to all five of these men, and they were all instantly healed and could both hear and speak.

Immediately, the minister stopped the meeting and began taking up an offering. He knew he would be able to get a large offering because of the mighty demonstration of God's power. People from all over the meeting ran to give him money because of these miraculous healings.

Some people would give large sums of money to be healed. But healing can't be bought; Jesus already paid for it on Calvary. This man used his ministry and, really, the healing power of God to obtain money in a wrong way. What happened to this minister? This character weakness, as well as other faults he didn't correct, eventually cost him not only his ministry, but his life.

In the first vision when Jesus appeared to me in Rockwall, Texas, one of the things He said to me was, "There are two things to be careful of. Number one, be sure you always give all the honor and the glory for everything that happens unto Me and unto My Name.

"Secondly, be very careful about money. Many on whom I've placed My Spirit and called unto such a ministry and anointed have become money-minded and have lost the anointing."

No minister should use his position for personal gain. *The Amplified Bible* makes the issue of ministers and money even more clear.

> 1 TIMOTHY 3:3,8 (*Amplified*)
> 3 ... not a lover of money — insatiable for wealth and ready to obtain it by QUESTIONABLE MEANS....

8 . . . not greedy for base gain — craving wealth and RESORTING TO IGNOBLE and DISHONEST METHODS of getting it.

That's one reason I tell folks, "Be careful about these people who prophesy money out of your pocket into their own. Leave them alone." Ministers can take up offerings, of course, and let people know about a need, but they should never make an issue of money. No minister should ever use his high calling in Christ for personal gain.

In my ministry, I've tried to say as little as possible about money. I don't believe we should emphasize money. I just believe if I feed the people, they will feed me, and God will provide. Actually, a minister of the gospel should be interested in building up the Kingdom of God, not in using money for his own personal gain.

Gordon Lindsay talks about ministers and money in his book, *Apostles, Prophets and Governments:*

Judas, one of the original Twelve who shared their ministry, disqualified himself and also destroyed his own soul by using his position for personal gain. . . .

A true apostle must be above even the suspicion of a covetous spirit. He may, in the interest of the Kingdom, become responsible for the handling of large sums of money, as the apostles were when the multitude sold their possessions and laid them at the apostles' feet (Acts 4:34-37). But he will be a faithful steward and will not lavish on himself money given to the cause of Christ for the work of the Kingdom. The story of Judas, given such prominence in the Scriptures, is of deep significance. [1]

Ministers of the gospel, including apostles, must be above reproach in every area, including how they handle money and how they obtain it.

Not a Novice

Another qualification for the apostolic office and for ministry in general is that a minister should *not* be a novice. In First Timothy 3:6, Paul said not to put a novice in authority: *"Not a novice, lest being lifted up with pride he fall into the condemnation of the devil"* (1 Tim. 3:6).

A novice is a new Christian or one who is young and undeveloped in spiritual things. Many folks could have been saved for many years, but they would still be novices if they haven't developed spiritually.

Why shouldn't a novice be put in a position of authority such as the apostolic office? A minister and his ministry must be proved first, and only then can he be used fully by God.

Talking about the ministry of a deacon, Paul said, *". . . let these also first be proved; then let them use the office of a deacon, being found blameless"* (1 Tim. 3:10). A deacon is a helper. If a helper needs to be proved, it stands to reason that an apostle who stands in an office of greater responsibility would also need to be proved.

That's why I get amused at these young fellows who run around saying, "I'm an apostle" or "I'm a prophet"! They are no more apostles and prophets than I'm last year's bird nest! God is not going to violate His own Word and make Himself out to be a liar by putting novices in an office of spiritual authority and oversight.

I had an experience with a so-called apostle when I was preaching once down in Texas. I was only about thirty years old at the time, but I had been in the ministry for many years, preaching, teaching, and laying hands on the sick.

There was a twenty-year-old fellow who called himself an apostle because some so-called prophet had laid hands on him and supposedly *made* an apostle out of him. The prophet supposedly *put* him into the apostolic office!

This young fellow taught that because he was an apostle, he had authority over all the other ministry gifts in the Body of Christ. So he came to me and said, "Since I'm an apostle, I have authority over you. I'll tell you where to go to hold meetings and where to preach. I'll arrange your schedule for you."

That fellow wasn't even a preacher, much less an apostle! He couldn't even call hogs, much less preach!

I said to him, "Oh? How many churches have you started?"

This so-called apostle answered, "I haven't started any churches."

He couldn't even build a chicken coop, much less start a church! Have you ever noticed that some of these so-called apostles want to come in and take over someone else's work, but they don't want to pay the price to pioneer a work of their own! They aren't apostles; they are false apostles — certainly not New Testament apostles!

"Why," I said to him, "you are no more an apostle than I'm an astronaut!"

Then he said to me, "You're in rebellion because you won't get under my authority! I'm going to cast that spirit of rebellion out of you."

I didn't need anything cast out of me. A man who says things like that needs something *taken* out of him — *ignorance* — and the teaching of the Word will do that.

You see, when this so-called prophet had laid hands on this fellow and supposedly made an apostle out of him, the "apostle" got all elated and lifted up in spiritual pride. Because he was a novice, he didn't have the spiritual wisdom and maturity to discern sound doctrine, so he fell into the condemnation and snare of the devil.

Weymouth's translation says a minister ". . . ought not to be a new convert for fear he should be blinded with pride and come under the same condemnation as the devil." Usually folks who go around declaring themselves to be apostles or prophets are lifted up in pride. They want to be an apostle because they think that gives them authority over the other ministry gifts.

That is the reason people ought to reach some age and accountability before they are ordained to the ministry. Any minister can go buy some ordination from one of those fly-by-night organizations. But they are not ordained biblically.

A minister of the gospel ought to want to be associated with a ministerial organization that not only has dignity, but is honorable and scriptural in ordaining its ministers — one that requires some qualifications for ordination.

A Good Report

1 TIMOTHY 3:7
7 Moreover he must have A GOOD REPORT OF THEM WHICH ARE WITHOUT; lest he fall into reproach and the snare of the devil.

Standing in any ministry office is a serious matter. One must have a good report resulting from his blameless character and conduct.

I want you to notice something the Bible says in the Book of James: *"My brethren, be not many masters, knowing that we shall receive the greater condemnation"* (James 3:1).

The word "master" here can also be translated *teacher. The Amplified Bible* makes this clear.

JAMES 3:1 *(Amplified)*
1 Not many [of you] should become teachers [self-constituted censors and reprovers of others], my brethren, for you know that we [teachers] will be JUDGED BY A HIGHER STANDARD AND WITH GREATER SEVERITY [than other people]. Thus we assume the greater accountability and the more condemnation.

I don't believe this only refers to teachers. It is true

concerning every ministry gift, including the apostolic office. Every ministry gift will be judged by a higher standard. And because we will be *judged* by a higher standard, we should *set* a higher standard in our character and conduct. Every minister should have a good report even by those who are not saved.

It is an awesome responsibility to be called to stand in the apostolic office, or any ministry office for that matter. We can only fulfill our ministries with the help of the Holy Spirit. The *call* and the spiritual *equipment* have to do with the inward man. But we can see that the *qualifications* to the ministry have to do with the outward man.

God has done something with the inward man. He has fulfilled His part by placing the call in man's spirit and by giving him the spiritual equipment to fulfill that call. But the minister must present his body — the outward man — as a living sacrifice in order to qualify himself to stand worthy of such a high calling in Christ Jesus.

> **JAMES 3:2 (*Amplified*)**
> 2 For we all often stumble and fall and offend in many things. And if anyone does not offend in speech — never says the wrong things — he is a fully developed character and a perfect man, able to control his whole body and to curb his entire nature.

Moffatt's translation says, "In many things we all stumble." The footnote in the *Moffatt* translation says, "Imperfections characterize man." None of us is perfected yet, but we should all be moving toward maturity in Christ.

If any minister has fallen behind in any of these areas, he needs to repent and ask God to forgive him. Then he needs to see to it that he perfects himself in these areas. Every ministry gift should be a guide and an example in Christian conduct and character.

Be Faithful To Prepare Yourself

If God calls you to be an apostle, *He* will supernaturally equip you. But you won't start out in that office anyway. God has His ways of doings things. You just need to prepare yourself so God can use you in any way He desires. The Bible says, *"Study to shew thyself approved unto God, a workman that needeth not to be ashamed, rightly dividing the word of truth"* (2 Tim. 2:15).

Although you won't be able to enter immediately into the ministry God has for you, you can prepare yourself through studying the Word and preparing your heart. You can do your part. Preparation time is never wasted time.

If you are faithful in the time of preparation to study God's Word to show yourself approved, in God's time, step by step, He will move you into the ministry He eventually has for you. As you are faithful to prepare yourself, He will be faithful to open doors for ministry.

You must also prepare yourself for your high calling in Christ by separation from the things of the world that hold you back from the things of God. Sometimes you need to lay aside those things that are not necessarily sin, but they take up valuable time. The Lord is looking for those who will dedicate and consecrate themselves wholly unto Him for His use.

It is as we present our bodies as living sacrifices and renew our minds with the Word of God that God can use us fully. The Bible says, ". . . *Walk in the Spirit, and ye shall not fulfil the lust of the flesh*" (Gal. 5:16). And ". . . *he that soweth to his flesh shall of the flesh reap corruption; but he that soweth to the Spirit shall of the Spirit reap life everlasting*" (Gal. 6:8).

If you are faithful to study God's Word and to serve Him right where you are, God will set you into the Body of Christ and promote you as *He* desires. But remember this: *Don't get taken up with names and titles.* If you have to tell folks you are an apostle or a prophet, then you probably aren't one. You don't have to go around telling everyone you are a man or a woman, do you? You are born that way and it's evident to everyone.

The same thing ought to be true over in the spiritual realm. If you are called to the ministry, it ought to be readily distinguishable what you are and what your call is. You shouldn't have to go around telling people what your calling is by giving yourself titles and labels. People will know what you are by your spiritual equipment and endowments.

And if you don't know what God has called you to do, just be faithful to serve Him right where you are. Be faithful in your local church, study His Word, and leave the rest up to God.

Also, remember this: *God rewards faithfulness. He doesn't reward offices.* An apostle or prophet won't receive any more reward than anyone else who is faithful to do what God has called him to do. Higher offices do not receive any more reward; there is just a greater responsibility that goes along with the office.

That's why it's important for you to be faithful to fulfill the responsibilities God has given *you* because *God rewards faithfulness*!

---

[1]Lindsay, pp. 18,19.

SECTION II

PROPHETS

Chapter 5

The Office of the Prophet Contrasted in Old and New Testaments

> . . . *When he* [Jesus] *ascended up on high, he led captivity captive, and gave gifts unto men.* . . .
>
> *And he gave some, APOSTLES; and some, PROPHETS; and some, EVANGELISTS; and some, PASTORS and TEACHERS.*
> — Ephesians 4:8,11

Over the years, Jesus has appeared to me several times, and each time He instructed me about ministry relative to the Church. In these visitations, He explained to me that His plans for the Church under the New Covenant are different than His dealings were with Israel under the Old Covenant.

People under the Old Covenant were not born again. God could not deal with them *in the Spirit* because their spirits hadn't been recreated and born again. But under the New Covenant, our spirits have been recreated in the image and likeness of God, so God can deal with us *in the Spirit* as born-again *children* of God.

Therefore, God's plan for the Church — the Body of Christ — under the New Covenant is different in several respects from those living under the Old Covenant.

For example, His plan for the Church *in ministry* is different under the New Covenant than it was under the Old Covenant. God deals with the Church — the Body of Christ — differently in ministry than He did with the Israelites who were not born again.

The Prophet Under the Old Covenant

In this chapter, I will share with you what Jesus said to me about the differences between the office of the prophet under the Old Covenant and under the New Covenant.

The first occasion Jesus talked to me about the office of the prophet occurred in 1959. In that vision, the Lord talked to me for an hour and a half about the prophet's ministry. (For a complete account of this vision, please *see* Rev. Kenneth E. Hagin's book, *I Believe in Visions.*) Then Jesus also appeared to me in 1987 and talked to me about the offices of the apostle and the prophet and about the local church.

In the 1959 vision, Jesus said to me, "There is a difference between the Old Testament prophet and the New Testament prophet. That is where many folks miss it today. They try to give the New Testament prophet the same status as the Old Testament prophet, and he doesn't have the same status.

"First of all," Jesus said, "the Old Testament prophet was the only *ministry* in operation from the standpoint of preaching or teaching the people by inspired utterance. That's not true under the New Testament. Under the New Covenant, I have set the *fivefold* ministry in the Church for the perfecting of the saints" (Eph. 4:11,12).

"Not only that, but under the New Covenant every believer is to follow the Holy Spirit for himself [Rom. 8:14]. Under the Old Covenant there was a sacrificial system for worship because God was dealing with spiritually dead people; they couldn't worship God in *spirit* and in truth.

"But under the New Covenant, believers are not to set up some kind of a system for believers to worship God or to communicate with Him. Believers are to worship God in Spirit and in truth, and they are to be led by their spirit.

"Under the Old Testament," Jesus continued, "the only people who were specially anointed by God were the prophet, priest, and king. The king was anointed by the Holy Ghost to stand in that office, but he was not anointed to *preach*. The priest was anointed by the Holy Ghost to stand in that office, but he wasn't a preacher either. He taught the Law to the people so they would obey God's commandments and precepts. But he wasn't a preacher.

"Of course," Jesus continued, "the priests had a ministry under the Old Covenant. But it was not necessarily a ministry of *preaching* and *teaching*. They did exhort the people about the ways of the Lord and about carrying out the sacrificial system. But, actually, under the Old Covenant the prophets were the only *preachers* or *ministers* the people had. The prophet was the only one who could speak for God, as he was inspired by the Holy Spirit.

"You notice how the prophets kept preaching to Israel, trying to get the people to turn back to God. Even in the Old Testament, the prophet was a preacher, and he preached by inspired utterance."

Jesus continued, "Under the Old Testament, what we call the laity or the laymen didn't have the Holy Ghost. The Holy Ghost came upon the prophet, priest, and king to anoint them to stand in those offices. But the layman didn't have the Holy Spirit upon him.

"Remember David was prophet, priest, and king [Acts 2:25,30; 2 Sam. 5:12; 24:25]. No one else but the prophet, priest, and king had the Holy Spirit in any measure *upon* them. The only exception to that was when God would sometimes call people to carry out special jobs or functions for Him. Then He would anoint them with the Holy Spirit just to perform that task."

In reading the Scriptures, very often it says that God *anointed* or *empowered* someone with the Spirit, and it was just to do a particular job for Him. For example, when God wanted Gideon to save Israel from the hand of the Midianites, He anointed Gideon just to do that (*see* Judges chapter 6).

But Gideon didn't have the Holy Spirit dwelling *in* him to lead him, so he could only follow God in the natural realm. That's why he wasn't sure whether it was God or not who was dealing with him. He put out a fleece before God to make sure it was really God leading him

(Judges 6:36-40). God wasn't *in* Gideon's spirit because Gideon wasn't born again, so God had to lead him through the flesh in the natural realm.

Jesus explained all this to me. And then in the vision, Jesus said to me, "Very seldom under the New Covenant does God ever lead anyone through the flesh. When He does, it is only when people are so spiritually insensitive and dull that they would not understand His leading any other way."

Jesus pointed out that in the New Testament, it says, *"For as many as are led by the Spirit of God, they are the sons of God"* (Rom. 8:14). It doesn't say that as many as are led by fleeces or through the flesh in the natural realm are the sons of God.

Under the Old Covenant, people couldn't be led by their spirits, and they couldn't approach God for themselves. They had to approach God through the priest. They had to bring a sacrifice and an offering, and no one could enter the Holy of Holies where the Presence of God was kept shut up, except the High Priest. And the High Priest did so only with great precaution. If anyone else intruded into the Holy of Holies, he fell dead instantly.

Jesus said to me, "Under the Old Covenant, the prophet gave guidance to the people because they didn't have the Holy Ghost for themselves. So the people had to go to the prophet to inquire what 'Thus saith the Lord.'"

The Prophet Under the New Covenant

"But under the New Covenant," Jesus continued, "I

didn't put the prophet in that office to lead or guide believers. Every believer has the Holy Spirit *in him* to lead and guide him; each believer can hear from God for himself. Therefore, under the New Covenant, it is unscriptural to seek guidance through a prophet."

Jesus said, "Sometimes in His own divine sovereignty, God may speak a word to a person through a prophet to confirm something a believer already has in his own spirit. But the prophet is not to lead or guide people through that office; normally every believer will be led by the Holy Spirit through his *own* spirit.

"Sons of God can *expect* to be led by the Spirit of God [Rom. 8:14]. Therefore, the number one way the Holy Spirit leads all Christians, including prophets, is by the inward witness.

"Secondly, the Holy Spirit leads believers by the still, small voice. And, thirdly, believers are led by the authoritative Voice of the Holy Ghost in their own spirit.

"Then, fourthly," Jesus said, "very rarely, but once in a while as He wills, the Holy Spirit may occasionally lead people by a vision or a revelation. Of course, that happens more frequently to those who are called to the office of the prophet."

You see, under the New Covenant, we have a better covenant based upon better promises (Heb. 8:6), and we don't need to seek direction for our lives from anyone but God. Jesus is our High Priest. The Book of Hebrews tells us that Jesus entered in once and for all with His blood to obtain an eternal redemption for us (Heb. 9:12). And because believers are born again, they can be led by the Holy Spirit in their own spirit (Rom. 8:14).

Jesus also explained that under the New Covenant, all believers are made kings and priests unto God (1 Peter 2:9; Rev. 5:9,10). In other words, all believers have access to God for themselves; they don't have to go through a priest or a sacrificial system to get to God. They don't have to go through an intermediary of any kind — even a person who stands in a ministry office — in order to get to God or to receive His counsel and guidance.

Of course, the pastor has the oversight of the flock (Acts 20:28). But believers don't have to go through their pastor to get their prayers answered or to be able to communicate with God. The pastor is just a spiritual overseer to help believers in the local body, and he is anointed by the Holy Ghost to stand in that office. But believers don't have to inquire of God through Him.

Jesus said, "Of course, there is a similarity in the ministries of the Old and New Testament prophets. For example, one characteristic of the prophet under the Old Covenant is that they were called seers because they would see into the realm of the spirit and see and know things supernaturally.

"That is also true of prophets under the New Covenant; they see and know things supernaturally. The revelation gifts such as the word of knowledge or the word of wisdom often operate with the gift of discerning of spirits."

The gift of the word of knowledge is a supernatural revelation by the Spirit of God concerning certain facts in the mind of God — facts about people, places, or things in the *past* or *present*.

The word of wisdom is supernatural revelation into events that will occur in the *future*, or about the plans and purposes of God. The discerning of spirits enables prophets to see and hear in the realm of the spirit.

Schools of Prophets

In a vision in 1959, Jesus also told me another major difference between the prophet under the Old Covenant and under the New Covenant.

Jesus explained, "Under the Old Testament, since the prophets were the only ministers the people had, it was scriptural to have schools where they could be trained.

"But under the New Covenant," Jesus explained, "My plan for the New Testament Church *in ministry* is different than it was under the Old Covenant. That's why I set the fivefold ministry in the Church. You see, all the ministries need the same basic training."

Jesus said, "One reason it is unscriptural under the New Testament to have schools of prophets is that it leaves the impression that prophets are the only ministry gift there is under the New Covenant, or the most important one, and they aren't.

"Under the New Testament, it is scriptural to have schools for *ministers* because all the ministry gifts need the same basic training. The prophet doesn't need different *basic* training from the other ministry gifts. Then once ministry gifts receive the same fundamental training, let Me separate each of them unto the ministry I have called them to" (*see* Acts 13:2).

Jesus continued, "There are some things the prophet needs to be taught, just as there are some things the apostle, evangelist, pastor, and teacher need to be taught. But, basically, the same *principles*, *training*, and *qualifications* that apply to the prophet, apply to all the ministry gifts. It is *ministerial* training."

Before the Lord explained this to me, I had thought about having a school of prophets. But then He explained this to me, and that's the reason we started RHEMA Bible *Training* Center — not a school of prophets.

What happens so many times is that people try to carry over Old Testament practices into the New Testament, when we are under a different covenant altogether. We are under a *better* covenant established on *better* promises (Heb. 8:6).

Ranks or Classes of Prophets

In the 1987 visitation, Jesus explained about the different levels, ranks, or classes in each of the ministry gifts. And He explained this to me from the Scriptures.

Jesus said there are different ranks or classes in the prophetic office, just as there are in all the ministry gifts. There were foundational prophets, such as Paul, who established New Testament doctrine. We don't have prophets today in that rank or class.

Many think that the office of prophet passed away

with the prophets of the Early Church. They don't realize that that office is still in operation. However, prophets of our day are in a different rank or class than prophets of the Old Testament or the foundational prophets of the Early Church.

The prophet in the rank or class in the Church today does not add foundational doctrine to the Scriptures. As a ministry gift, he is to *edify* and *build up* the Body of Christ, of course. A prophet can illuminate the Word to the Body of Christ, sharing insights which make it relevant for today. But he's not to add new *doctrine* to the foundation of the New Testament.

Foundational prophets in the Early Church brought forth the revelation of the mystery of Christ — the gospel. Paul is an example of such a prophet. Then in the Early Church there were also prophets of a lesser rank or class, such as Agabus, who did not lay *doctrinal* foundation.

For example, Agabus brought forth revelation of a drought that was coming (Acts 11:28). The Holy Spirit warned the Church of things to come through Agabus, but that wasn't a revelation of doctrine adding to the foundation of the gospel.

Measures of Anointing

Jesus also told me in the 1987 visitation that there are different *degrees* or *levels of anointing* to those standing in the fivefold ministry offices. The *anointing* upon a person for ministry refers to the *empowering* and *equipping* of the Holy Spirit upon a person, enabling him to stand in a ministry office.

Jesus said it is possible for those who are called to these ministry offices to operate on different levels of anointing; some operate with a greater anointing and some with a lesser anointing in a given ministry office.

For example, we've all seen evangelists who are more anointed than others, or pastors or teachers who were more anointed than others. Also, sometimes people in ministry gift offices operate on a lower level of anointing when they first start out in ministry, but as they prove faithful to what God has called them to do, God moves them up to a higher level of anointing.

Jesus said that the same thing is true with the prophet. There are not only different classes of prophets, but within a given rank or class of prophetic office, there are also different measures of anointing to those standing in that office. In other words, one called to be a prophet could be more or less anointed to stand in that office.

The Bible talks about measures of anointing.

JOHN 3:34
34 For he whom God hath sent [Jesus] speaketh the words of God: for God giveth not the Spirit BY MEASURE unto him.

The Holy Spirit was given to Jesus *without* measure. The rest of us in the Body of Christ only have the Holy Spirit *by* measure or *in* a measure (Rom. 12:3).

Jesus also gave me Hebrews 2:4 and talked to me about "gifts" or *distributions* of the Holy Ghost.

HEBREWS 2:4
**4   God also bearing them witness, both with signs
and wonders, and with divers miracles, and
GIFTS OF THE HOLY GHOST, according to his
own will.**

For years I thought *"gifts* of the Holy Ghost" in this
verse referred to the nine gifts of the Spirit mentioned
in First Corinthians 12.

1 CORINTHIANS 12:4,7
**4   Now there are diversities of GIFTS, but the
same Spirit. . . .**
7   But the MANIFESTATION [or gift] **of the Spirit
is given to every man to profit withal.**

But Hebrews 2:4 couldn't mean spiritual gifts. God
had already borne them witness with signs, wonders,
and diverse miracles — referring to spiritual gifts.

But notice the word "and" in Hebrews 2:4. It is a
conjunction, and it means that something else is added
besides spiritual gifts. In other words, God bore them
witness with spiritual gifts *plus* something else.

In the margin of my Bible, the reference by the word
"gifts" in Hebrews 2:4 says *"distributions"* of the Holy
Ghost.

The word for "gifts" used in First Corinthians 12:4,7,
is "charisma," indicating a *spiritual gift.*

Gifts or *distributions* in Hebrews 2:4 is referring to
the fivefold ministry gifts listed in Ephesians 4:8-11:
apostles, prophets, evangelists, pastors, and teachers.

Therefore, we could read this verse: "God bearing
them witness both with signs, wonders, diverse mira-

cles, AND *distributions* of the Holy Ghost."

The gift or *distribution* of the Holy Spirit is the divine endowment or equipment upon a person which enables him to stand in a ministry office. God *distributes* the Holy Ghost to those called as ministry gifts, enabling and equipping them to carry out that function to the Body of Christ.

Distributions of the Holy Spirit are not upon laymen, because laymen do not stand in ministry gift offices. The layman does not have the distribution, the anointing, or the divine equipment of the Holy Spirit upon him to stand in a fivefold ministry office.

Notice in Hebrews 2:4 that it is "distribution*s*," of the Holy Spirit. The word is plural because there are measures of anointings even in these various offices. That is what Jesus told me. A person could be *more* or *less* anointed to stand in a particular ministry office.

Let's go to the Old Testament to further demonstrate that there are measures of anointing, because the Bible says, *". . . in the mouth of two or three witnesses every word may be established"* (Matt. 18:16).

Even in the Old Testament, there were prophets who had a greater anointing to stand in that office. Because of an increased anointing, the prophetic ministry of some Old Testament prophets was more widely known and more far reaching than others.

We find a reference to *measures of anointing* in Second Kings chapter 2. God had told Elijah to anoint Elisha to be prophet in his "room," or in his stead or place.

2 KINGS 2:9
9   And it came to pass, when they were gone over,
that Elijah said unto Elisha, Ask what I shall do
for thee, before I be taken away from thee. And
Elisha said, I pray thee, let a DOUBLE PORTION
of thy spirit be upon me.

Elisha received a double portion or a double *measure of anointing* to stand in the office of the prophet than Elijah had upon him. And if you'll study the Scriptures, you'll find that signs and wonders in Elisha's ministry were about double to those operating in Elijah's ministry. You can readily see that a person could be more or less anointed to stand in an office.

If you are called to the full-time ministry, you will have to stand in your office and minister according to the measure or distribution of the Holy Spirit given to you. However, the anointing on a person's life can be increased by faithfulness, consecration, and diligence in the Word of God and prayer.

Chapter 6
What Is a
New Testament Prophet?

A prophet is a *ministry gift* given by God to the Church. No one can *make* himself a prophet or *call* himself to be a prophet. *God* alone calls and set prophets in the Church. There is an anointing on that office and the spiritual equipment of the Holy Spirit which enable a person to fulfill that function to the Body of Christ.

However, some folks get off-course doctrinally by thinking that a prophet's only function is to prophesy to people. That is only a small part of his ministry.

First and Foremost —
A Preacher or Teacher of the Word

Actually, a prophet's primary purpose and main ministry is to preach or teach the Word, or to be *both* a teacher and a preacher of the Word. Prophesying is *not* the main thrust of the prophet's ministry.

Even the prophets of the Old Testament were first preachers. They were constantly preaching to the people and calling them to repentance, because much of the time the Israelites were backslidden and out of God's will. So the prophets spoke to the people in behalf of God by prophetic inspiration.

Of course, you understand that under the New Testament, prophets aren't the only preachers or teachers of the Word. The foremost ministry of *any* of the ministry gifts is to preach or to teach.

We see this in Jesus' ministry, who stood in all five of the ministry offices. Notice why Jesus said the Holy Spirit was given to Him: *"The Spirit of the Lord is upon me, because he hath ANOINTED ME to PREACH THE GOSPEL . . ."* (Luke 4:18). One of the reasons Jesus was anointed was to preach.

> **MATTHEW 9:35**
> **35 And Jesus went about all the cities and villages, TEACHING in their synagogues, and PREACHING the gospel of the kingdom, and HEALING every sickness and every disease among the people.**

Even as a prophet, Jesus' ministry consisted, first, of *teaching*. Second, *preaching*. And third, *healing*. Anyone who is called to the fivefold ministry — apostle, prophet, evangelist, pastor, or teacher — is first called to preach or to teach the gospel.

To "preach" means *to proclaim* or *to tell*. To "teach" means *to expound* or *to explain*. Therefore, the ministry gifts are preachers or teachers because they either proclaim or explain the gospel in one respect or another. Their main function is to *preach* or *teach* the Word of God because that matures the saints and equips them for service.

Is the prophet supposed to prophesy? Yes, but that is not his main ministry. Study Jesus' prophetic ministry in the gospels. We do see spiritual gifts operating through Him, of course.

For example, He had a word of knowledge for the woman at the well (John 4:18). Jesus used the word of knowledge to convict a sinner of a need for a Savior. And we see the gift of working of miracles (John 2:3-11), and gifts of healings in operation in His ministry (Mark 5:25-34).

As a prophet, Jesus saw and knew things supernaturally (Luke 5:22; John 1:47). However, in His prophetic ministry, Jesus didn't go around prophesying to everyone He met.

But the Bible tells us what Jesus did do. He "... *went about all the cities and villages, TEACHING ... and PREACHING THE GOSPEL of the kingdom ...*" (Matt. 9:35).

Paul was also a prophet. Study his prophetic ministry. Paul was a foundational prophet because he wrote a large part of the New Testament, and it was revealed to him by the Holy Spirit (Eph. 3:3). But even as a prophet of that rank, Paul did not go around prophesying to everyone he met.

Even though Paul was an apostle and a prophet, he considered himself first a preacher of the gospel.

1 TIMOTHY 2:7
7   Whereunto I am ordained a PREACHER, and an APOSTLE, (I speak the truth in Christ, and lie not;) a TEACHER of the Gentiles in faith and verity.

2 TIMOTHY 1:11
11 Whereunto I am appointed a PREACHER, and an APOSTLE, and a TEACHER of the Gentiles.

In these cases where Paul mentions his ministry, he puts his preaching ministry first.

So a prophet can either be a preacher or a teacher, or both a preacher and a teacher of the gospel. Some folks only operate in the *preaching* ministry of the prophet; others operate only in the *teaching* ministry of the prophet. And some people operate in *both* the preaching and the teaching ministry of the prophet.

Paul operated in both the preaching and the teaching ministry of the prophet (1 Tim. 2:7; 2 Tim. 1:11).

On the other hand, John the Baptist, for example, who was also a prophet, operated in the *preaching* ministry of the prophet (Matt. 3:1). We know John was a prophet because Jesus called him a prophet: *". . . Among those that are born of women there is not a greater PROPHET than John the Baptist . . ."* (Luke 7:28).

As a prophet, John preached repentance, speaking by the inspiration of the Holy Spirit. Everywhere he went, he proclaimed the message of God to the people to repent and turn to God (Matt. 3:2). Repentance was his prophetic message to the people.

The prophet not only *preaches* the Word under the inspiration of the Holy Spirit, but he can also *teach* the Word by inspiration too.

Very often people say to me, "When you teach, it seems there is a different anointing besides just the teaching anointing." That's because I very often teach inspirationally by the prophetic anointing. The person who is strictly a teacher teaches with the teaching anointing to explain and instruct the people by precept and example, and that's the only anointing he has.

A prophet differs from the teacher in that the teacher speaks from a logical standpoint to explain, teach, and expound upon the Word. Sometimes the prophet is not so logical, even from a mental standpoint.

Speaking under the inspiration of the moment, the utterance the prophet gives appeals to the *spirit* of man. And sometimes his messages given by inspiration at the spur of the moment may not seem to fit with the rest of his message.

Of course, the prophet also has gifts of the Spirit which operate through him and equip him to stand in that office.

And we know from Paul's ministry that a person can stand in more than one office, as he is called and equipped by God. Paul stood in the offices of the apostle, prophet, and teacher.

But the point I'm trying to make is that teaching and preaching the Word is the major part of a prophet's ministry, not giving out personal messages.

You can readily see where some folks have missed it today. Many people have strange notions about what a New Testament prophet is. They build spiritual air castles or false ideas of what they think the prophet *ought* to be, which don't have any basis in Scripture.

Many think the prophet ought to go around giving out personal messages all the time, leading and guiding people by that office. Many people do that and call themselves prophets. We have an outbreak of this every so often in the Body of Christ; it isn't anything new.

For example, years ago I knew a number of couples who got married because some so-called prophet prophesied to them, telling them they should marry. Every single one of those marriages failed because they looked to a so-called prophet to guide them instead of the Holy Spirit residing within. Don't marry someone just because some so-called prophet prophesies to you.

For example, forty years ago one fellow I knew married a woman because someone prophesied that he should. It wasn't God's will, and it got him offtrack with God. He's been out of the ministry all these years and just recently got back in the ministry God had for him all those years. People are in danger when they go around trying to regulate other people's lives from the prophet's office.

I remember one fellow I knew several years ago who was called to the office of the prophet. But he got off into error because he thought he should prophesy all the time; he put prophesying before the Word! He had a message for practically everyone he met. He'd even stop people on the street to give them a "word" from God.

He didn't have a message from God for all those people! I tried to help him and tell him about the scriptural operation of prophetic office, but he wouldn't listen.

God had mightily used him at one time when he was walking in the light of the Word. One of my own board members told me how God had used this prophet in his own life.

This board member was in one of this prophet's meetings. The board member told me, "That man didn't know a thing about me. But suddenly in the middle of his sermon, he stopped, pointed to me, and said, 'Come up here.' Then he told me exactly what was wrong with me physically, laid hands on me, and I was instantly healed."

God had used this prophet mightily along that line. Later I had an opportunity to meet him because we were both staying in this board member's home for a short time. Every few minutes this "prophet" would prophesy to me. He had been in the house about twenty minutes, and he prophesied to me nineteen times! I didn't pay any attention to it. Not a word of it was so.

I told him, "You've distorted the office of the prophet. It's not what you think it is. The prophet doesn't just go around giving personal prophecies to everyone. He is first and foremost a preacher or a teacher of the Word of God."

But he wouldn't listen to me. He even tried to give personal messages to every church member in every church where he preached! He did that even when the Holy Spirit wasn't manifesting Himself through prophecy. In other words, he did it in the flesh, and evil spirits began to accommodate him and speak through him.

As this man's ministry got further and further from God, he began to prophesy money out of people's pockets into his. You'd better watch out for those ministers who are always talking about money.

When any so-called prophet starts prophesying about money — watch out! They aren't doing it by the

Spirit of God. Sooner or later they will get into trouble
because that isn't scriptural. You can't find that in the
Bible.

This man was misled about the true function of the
prophetic office. By misconstruing and misusing the
prophet's office, he went bankrupt spiritually. He finally
died at an early age. It's a pity because he could have
been such a blessing to the Body of Christ.

We can see why it's so important to heed what Jesus
said to me in the vision: "The prophet is first of all a
preacher or a teacher. His main ministry is to preach or
teach the Word. Prophesying is *not* his main ministry."

A prophet who bases his ministry on personal
prophecy instead of on preaching or teaching the Word
will get into error and wreak havoc in the Body of
Christ.

Prophets Speak From
The Inspiration of the Moment

One of the elements of the prophet's ministry is
divinely inspired speaking, or speaking under the unction and power of the Holy Spirit on the inspiration of
the moment. This is true of both Old Testament and
New Testament prophets.

Actually, preaching can carry an element of prophecy
if it's by the inspiration of the Holy Spirit. *Prophecy* is
inspired utterance in a *known tongue*. *Preaching* can be
inspired utterance in a *known tongue* too. However, not
all preaching is prophesying.

The prophet often speaks by inspiration. In that sense, his preaching can be prophesying in its simple form — inspired utterance to edify, exhort, and comfort (1 Cor. 14:3).

The prophet prepares himself, but not quite like the other ministry gifts prepare themselves. Yes, he prepares himself in the Word. But he prepares himself more by praying and seeking God.

Actually, it's a preparation of the *heart* because the prophet has to prophesy according to the proportion of his faith (Rom. 12:6). Therefore, his faith has to be kept strong by spending much time with the Lord and in His Word. Then he speaks more from inspiration, under the prophetic unction, not from something he necessarily knows mentally.

Some evangelists are really operating in a measure in the prophet's office when their preaching is inspirational and given on the spur of the moment. To "prophesy" means *to speak for another*, and evangelists very often speak for God by the inspiration of the Holy Spirit.

On the other hand, many people we call evangelists are really *exhorters*. Exhorters are gifted in exhorting people to be saved and to walk with God. Romans 12:8 mentions exhorting as a ministry, but it is not a ministry gift.

True New Testament *evangelists* have miracles and gifts of healings operating in their ministry (1 Cor. 12:28). We can take our pattern of a New Testament evangelist from Philip the evangelist. Miracles and healings operated in his ministry (Acts 8:5-13).

However, even though the evangelist may operate in a measure in the prophetic office if he preaches by the inspiration of the Holy Spirit, the prophet's ministry also differs significantly from the evangelist's ministry.

For one thing, the evangelist knows what he is going to preach about. He preaches Christ and Him crucified. The evangelist brings forth the message of salvation and he stays right with that message. The teacher usually knows what he is going to teach about, too, and stays right with his message.

But the prophet may not know *what* his subject is until he gets up to speak. Also, the prophet has other revelation gifts of the Spirit operating in his ministry on a more consistent basis, while the evangelist and teacher do not.

The other ministry gifts, such as the pastor or teacher, can also speak by revelation from a sudden impulse of the moment. But speaking by the revelation of the moment with little or no forethought occurs more consistently and with greater frequency with the prophet. He speaks from the light of a sudden revelation at the moment. However, his subject is always the Word of God.

Of course, even the layman can speak under the inspiration of the Holy Spirit because Paul said, ". . . *ye may all prophesy one by one . . .*" (1 Cor. 14:31). Paul was evidently referring to a believers' meeting in this passage, where all the believers participated and brought forth a psalm, hymn, or spiritual song (Eph.

5:19; Col. 3:16) by the simple gift of prophecy.

Laymen can speak under inspiration by the simple gift of prophecy, which is inspired utterance for edification, exhortation, and comfort (1 Cor. 14:3). But speaking by the simple gift of prophecy doesn't make them prophets. Paul asked the question, *". . . are all prophets?"* (1 Cor. 12:29). Of course all people are *not* prophets.

I saw marvelous things happen in believers' meetings in the churches I pastored, as believers spoke by the simple gift of prophecy. Some of these people were uneducated; some couldn't even read or write, let alone speak eloquently.

But when the Holy Ghost came upon them, words of inspiration just came pouring out of their mouths. We would all sit there and weep as we heard the Holy Spirit speak through them. It was such a blessing to the congregation.

However, their inspired utterance was the simple gift of prophecy in operation. The prophet, on the other hand, could speak inspirationally in the simple gift of prophecy, or revelation gifts of the Spirit could also be in operation in his inspirational speaking.

I knew ministers in times past in the Pentecostal Movement who preached and taught the Word by inspired utterance. In other words, they preached and taught more from the prophet's office by inspired utterance than they did from extensive notes. They studied the Word and waited before God in prayer, but they very seldom prepared a message.

They preached and taught the Word largely by

inspiration. Sometimes they didn't know what they were going to say when they got up to speak, but the Holy Spirit gave it to them at the spur of the moment.

Smith Wigglesworth's ministry was a dramatic example of one who spoke by divinely inspired utterance. I never knew Wigglesworth personally, but I had the opportunity to hear Donald Gee talk about Wigglesworth's ministry in a ministers' meeting I attended.

Donald Gee said, "We always had Wigglesworth speak every year at our General Conference because we wanted our young preachers to see his prophetic ministry in operation.

"Wigglesworth had no formal education, so when he would start out preaching, he would stumble in his speech and was often hard to understand. But when the Spirit of God came upon him, he became a different person. He began preaching prophetically — inspired words just flowed out of his mouth."

The Assemblies of God wanted their young preachers to see that prophetic ministry in operation. It's interesting that Wigglesworth never called himself a prophet or an apostle. And yet there is no doubt that he stood in both offices because the characteristics of both offices were evident in his ministry.

I started preaching as a Baptist minister, and I always preached from notes. When I came over among Pentecostal preachers, in those days very few of them ever preached from notes. Many of them were more inspirational preachers. It was amazing how God used them as they preached by the inspiration of the Holy Spirit.

These Pentecostal preachers were standing in the prophet's office in a measure as they preached inspirationally. Of course they prepared beforehand. They studied the Word and waited before God in prayer, but sometimes they didn't know what their message was until they got up to speak. God gave it to them at the spur of the moment by the inspiration of the Holy Spirit.

Several years ago, the Lord spoke to me along this line, particularly about my night services. In the day services, I always taught. Teaching is more logical and follows a pattern. It's more line upon line, precept upon precept.

But the Lord said to me, "Don't prepare a sermon for the night services. Just spend your time praying and waiting before Me in prayer and by meditating in the Word, and I'll bring out of your spirit whatever that congregation needs. Don't worry if you don't have a message beforehand. I'll give it to you when you get up to speak."

So I began doing that. When I would get up to give my message, I would preach or teach by inspiration. Sometimes I don't know what my message is until I get up to speak. That is the prophet's office in demonstration. For example, sometimes I have the singers keep singing a little longer until I get it clear in my spirit which direction the Holy Spirit wants me to go.

Of course, there are those who would take this and get off into a ditch on one side of the road. They would think I'm saying, "You don't need to prepare; God will give you a message." I'm not saying that at all!

A prophet can't get up to preach or teach inspirational unless he has spent much time in preparation before the Lord. God can't pull the Word *out of* his spirit if a prophet hasn't spent time putting the Word *into* his spirit.

The Prophetic Office in Demonstration In Preaching and Teaching

As I said, many people have misunderstood the office of the prophet because they expect the prophet to always be prophesying over people. That is a minor part of the prophet's ministry.

Actually, the prophet's ministry is operating many times and dear folks don't recognize it. It is often in manifestation as he preaches and teaches prophetically to people's needs in his messages. The Holy Ghost directs him what to say, and it is exactly what the people need to hear.

For example, I get to preaching sometimes and say things spontaneously that I didn't know I was going to say, but I'm ministering to people prophetically in my message. The prophet's ministry is in operation, but folks miss it because they are waiting for the *spectacular* and they miss the *supernatural*.

The prophet can minister prophetically to the needs of the people in his messages because he is more sensitive to spiritual things and to the spiritual needs of the congregation. In this way, he is more sensitive to people's spiritual needs at the moment than either the evangelist or the teacher. He knows what the Holy Ghost wants to say and do in the people's midst.

For example, one time I was preaching in a certain place, and in the middle of my message, I jumped down off the platform preaching. I got right down in front of a certain couple, whom I found out later were preachers. I began teaching by inspiration of the Holy Spirit what the Bible says about the marriage relationship.

I didn't know why I had departed from my sermon to preach on that subject. But I found out later that this pastor's wife had begun thinking she was too spiritual to have sexual relations with her husband.

I had no way of knowing anything about that couple. But preaching like that under the inspiration of the Holy Spirit was actually the prophet's ministry in demonstration.

But then some folks say, "I thought Brother Hagin was a prophet, but all he does is preach and teach!" They don't understand the prophetic ministry in operation! That was an example of the prophet's ministry in operation, teaching the Word by inspired utterance of the Holy Spirit.

A prophet may even do or act out certain things, inspired by the Holy Spirit. It's God working through him in that office to minister supernaturally to people.

For example, some years ago I held a meeting in a certain church in Texas. The pastor told me, "I met with the board and told them, 'The Monday night offering will go to meet our expenses. Every other night will be

Brother Hagin's offering.' The board agreed to that."

One night during this meeting as I was preaching, I suddenly ran down off the platform and sat next to a fellow. I put my arm around him, and said to him, "Someone is trying to steal my offering. A certain board member called a board meeting and said, 'The guest speaker is getting too much money. Let's keep half of it.' A man like that is a thief. He might as well rob a filling station on the way home."

At the time, I didn't know why I was doing or saying that. It was the prophet's office in demonstration. But I noticed that the fellow turned every color but white. After I did that, I ran back to the platform and picked up my message right where I'd left off.

After the service, the pastor said to me, "Brother Hagin, the man you said that to was the very board member who had called the meeting and said, 'Brother Hagin is getting too much money. Let's keep half of it.'"

You see, the prophet's ministry was in operation, but folks didn't recognize it. In the natural, I had no knowledge that had transpired, or what the man had said in that board meeting. That was a word of knowledge operating in the prophet's office. And I had no idea I was going to say and do that; it happened by the inspiration of the Holy Spirit.

Similar things like that may occasionally happen with other ministry gifts, but they will occur more consistently in the prophet's office.

The Role of Music in the Prophetic Office

Music inspired by the Holy Spirit can often enhance the prophetic anointing. In the Old Testament, music played a crucial part in the prophet's ministry (2 Kings 3:15). When the minstrel played, the hand of the Lord moved upon the prophet. The hand of the Lord is the Holy Ghost.

Music can sometimes spiritually enhance the anointing that comes upon the prophet to minister prophetically. On the other hand, if he doesn't have the right music, it can hinder him. Some music is more spiritually inspiring than other music.

Many times when the Spirit of God is moving on me mightily, I don't need music to inspire me spiritually. I just get up and take off "prophesying" — preaching or teaching by inspired utterance.

But sometimes when the Holy Spirit is moving mightily, and someone sings or plays the wrong music, it can cause the anointing of the Holy Spirit to wane. On the other hand, if the music is spiritually inspiring, it can increase the anointing.

For example, I was holding a meeting at a certain church one time, and during the offering the orchestra played a particularly anointed song. The Spirit of God came upon me, and when I got up to preach, I was in the Spirit. The prophetic unction came upon me to prophesy, and I ministered by the Spirit for two hours.

Under that heavy anointing, I saw into the realm of the spirit. I ministered to several preachers prophetically. Through the word of knowledge, I heard in the

Spirit something one preacher in the audience had said to someone else days before. Then under the anointing of the Holy Spirit, I was able to minister supernaturally to that preacher.

Why don't I minister prophetically like that in every service? Because I can only minister that way as the Spirit wills. I'm not running things; I'm not the Head of the Church. And I'm not going to fabricate or conjure up something.

If the Holy Spirit doesn't move that way, there is nothing I can do to make it happen. That's how people get over into occult powers! *They* try to make something happen when the Holy Spirit isn't moving by the gifts of the Spirit.

It's not necessary to have a supernatural move of the Holy Spirit through the gifts of the Spirit in every service. If it were necessary, the Holy Spirit would demonstrate Himself that way because He's the One in charge who orchestrates the move of God's power.

But a prophet can get off-course spiritually thinking God is going to move by the gifts of the Spirit in every service. The Holy Spirit may or He may not; it's up to Him, not man.

The New Testament Prophet Is a Seer

Another element of the prophetic ministry is that the prophet is a seer. A *seer* is one who sees into the realm of the spirit through the gift of discerning of spirits. You see, a vision is a manifestation of the gift of discerning of spirits in operation.

The gift of discerning of spirits may also be accompanied by a word of wisdom or a word of knowledge. But the vision itself is the discerning of spirits in operation because it allows the prophet to *see* and *hear* in the realm of the spirit.

Many prophets in the Old Testament and the New Testament were seers. They had revelation gifts of the Spirit operating in their ministry on a more consistent basis.

The revelation gifts which qualify a prophet to stand in that office are the word of knowledge and/or the word of wisdom and the gift of discerning of spirits, plus prophecy.

Prophecy is necessary because it is the inspired utterance enabling the prophet to speak forth what the Lord has given him. I didn't think that up. Jesus told me that when He appeared to me in 1959 and talked to me about the prophet's office. (For further study *see* Rev. Kenneth E. Hagin's *The Ministry Gifts* and *The Holy Spirit and His Gifts*.)

Anyone could have a word of knowledge, a word of wisdom, or discerning of spirits operate in his life occasionally. But the prophet has the revelation gifts operating in his life on a more consistent basis.

Let me give you an example of seeing and hearing in the realm of the spirit and knowing things supernaturally by the prophet's office. I was preaching in a meeting and suddenly I saw into the realm of the spirit. It concerned a man in the congregation. I pointed to the man, and said, "If I miss it, just say, 'You missed it.'

"You are a pastor," I said to him. "I saw you stand-ing three days ago looking out the picture window in your office. Three things were bothering you. One of them was the finances of the church. Another was you wanted to leave the church. And the third problem was a domestic issue."

He said, "You are exactly right."

Then I just told him by the Spirit what the Lord said to do about each problem and how God would solve each one.

Now I want you to see something here. That certainly was revelation, wasn't it? That was a demonstration of the word of knowledge operating in conjunction with the gift of discerning of spirits in the prophet's office.

But even though it was revelation, it had nothing to do with adding to the doctrinal foundation of the New Testament. Prophets in our day may have something revealed to them, but it is *not* something which adds doctrinal foundation to the Bible. It will only build upon the foundation that has already been laid.

So a true New Testament prophet is first and fore-most a preacher or teacher of the Word. Second, he preaches or teaches by inspired utterance. Third, he has revelation gifts plus prophecy operating consis-tently in his life and ministry. Fourth, he is a seer; he sees into the realm of the Spirit as the Holy Spirit wills. These scriptural qualifications constitute the office of the New Testament prophet.

Chapter 7

Prophets Are Not To Guide and Direct New Testament Believers

As I said, in the 1959 vision, Jesus emphasized the role of the prophet under the New Covenant by explaining, "Under the New Covenant, I did not put prophets in the Church to *lead*, *guide*, or *direct* people's lives."

You can see how believers can wreak much havoc in their lives by going to a prophet for direction and guidance, because we are to be led by the Spirit of God (Rom. 8:14), not by prophets.

Directing the Lives of Others Is Fortune-telling

I know successful people who went bankrupt in business because they followed some so-called prophet's advice. Some of these people were very successful and had millions of dollars and beautiful, palatial mansions. But they lost everything by trying to follow the guidance of some so-called prophet.

For example, I was preaching in a certain state, and a wealthy businessman came to one of my meetings. I had met him once, and I knew he was wealthy, but I knew nothing else about him. But the minute he came into my meeting, the Lord spoke to me about him. At the Lord's direction, I later told him what the Lord had said to me.

This man owned a palatial home and several expensive cars and was very successful in business; he was worth millions of dollars. He had servants, a private plane, and his children drove brand-new expensive cars. But then he started going to a so-called prophetess for direction and counsel before he would make any business deal. The Lord told me that he was going to lose everything he owned if he kept listening to her.

Actually, people who try to direct other people's lives through the office of the prophet are nothing more than fortune-tellers. Many people don't have enough sense to know that. This woman tried to guide this man's business affairs through "spiritual gifts." But it wasn't the Holy Spirit that was in operation through her; she was nothing more than a fortune-teller.

In First Thessalonians 5:20,21, the Bible says, *"Despise not prophesyings. Prove all things; hold fast that which is good."* We aren't to despise prophesying. But on the other hand, we aren't supposed to believe everything everyone prophesies to us either. The Bible tells us to *prove* all things to see if they are of God.

This woman's counsel obviously wasn't of God. Believers trying to inquire about God's leading or direction in their lives through a prophet are on dangerous ground. This businessman should have had enough *common* sense to know that when every one of his business deals failed because of the advice of this "prophetess," her advice wasn't any good!

Besides, a businessman ought to have some *busi-*

ness sense! And if he needs direction in business, he should seek *God*'s counsel first. Then if he needs to, he could consult with others who have business expertise.

I told this businessman what the Lord told me to tell him — that he was going to lose everything if he didn't quit listening to that woman who claimed to be a prophetess. But some people hear only what they want to hear. He told someone I agreed with what he was doing. And he kept inquiring through that so-called prophetess until he lost everything he had and went bankrupt.

This businessman was so deceived, he wouldn't make a move in business without calling this woman. Some of these false prophets and prophetesses prey upon people to get their money. They are no more prophets and prophetesses than I'm an astronaut. But just because some people go off into error, that doesn't do away with the legitimate prophetic ministry.

The true prophet doesn't try to run people's lives through that office. A prophet needs to be very careful in the area of personal prophecy. That's why when I'm ministering to people through the prophetic office, I very often say to them, "Does that mean anything to you? Does that confirm what you already have in your own heart? If it doesn't bear witness with your own spirit, don't pay a bit of attention to it."

Prophets Who Open Themselves Up To Familiar Spirits

Because prophets weren't set in the Church to lead and guide people's lives, they will get off-course spiritually if they try to do it. They will open themselves up to occult powers and familiar spirits.

For example, I was holding a meeting in a certain city, staying in the home of a wealthy businessman who was a member of the church where I was ministering. This man owned a shopping center and was extremely successful in business.

This businessman asked me, "Brother Hagin, do you know So-and-so?" and mentioned a certain minister.

I didn't know the man personally, but I knew about him. I'm convinced the minister he was talking about was called of God and at one time walked uprightly before God in the ministry. But then he began yielding to wrong spirits.

This businessman said, "Our church helped sponsor this minister in a meeting here in town. Nearly every day this minister would come into my office and we'd talk or go out to lunch.

"I had an heirloom — a seven-carat diamond ring — that I'd inherited from my father, which I very seldom ever wore. I had it wrapped up in a handkerchief in the back right-hand corner of the chest of drawers in my bedroom.

"One day when this minister came into my office, he turned to me and said, 'You have a seven-carat diamond ring you inherited from your father. It's wrapped up in a handkerchief in the right-hand corner of the third drawer in your dresser. God said you are to get it, and give it to me.'"

That's supernatural knowledge, isn't it? It's not only supernatural knowledge, it's *spectacular* knowledge. But, remember, the devil operates in the supernatural realm too. You'd better watch those folks who prophesy rings off your fingers and money out of your pockets into theirs. Don't have anything to do with people like that.

The businessman said to me, "How did that minister know about that ring? I've never told anyone that. No human knew about that heirloom but me and my wife. Naturally I thought, *That must be God.* So I went home and got it, and brought it back and gave it to him.

"About a week later, the minister came into my office, and someone crossed him and made him mad, and he started cussing. The minister closed the meeting and left town. Shortly after he left town, two young men came to me, and said, 'While that man was in town, he got us off into homosexuality.' "

This businessman told me, "I thought to myself, *Dear Lord, I missed God! That man's not even walking with God. He's off into sin! And now he's got my diamond ring!*"

Shortly after that incident, I was holding a meeting for a pastor, and this same minister came to visit the pastor's church. This minister was used in spiritual gifts, and at one time he'd had a marvelous healing ministry. Doctors even attested to the supernatural healings and were amazed about them.

But, you see, if a minister isn't careful, he can get lifted up in pride when God uses him, and he can walk away from God and get into sin. Or he can get money-minded and lose the anointing of God.

Anyway, the pastor invited the minister to come up on the platform to say a few words to the congregation. I was sitting behind the minister on the platform as he addressed the congregation. Just as if someone were talking behind me, I heard the Holy Spirit say, "Occult powers. Familiar spirits." That's what was operating through him, and how he knew about that business-man's heirloom diamond ring!

About that time, a minister friend of mine called me and said, "That minister is in town preaching. He's telling everyone that he's a prophet. After the meeting, I confronted him and asked him, 'When you hear things in the spirit realm, how do you know you're listening to the right voice?'

"This minister answered, 'Well, I don't know whether I am or not. I just trust God that the voice speaking to me is God.'"

That's not only spiritually immature, that's danger-ous! A prophet better know the Voice of God!

Then my minister friend asked him, "How often is the voice accurate? All the time?"

He answered, "Oh, maybe eighty percent of the time it's right."

People like that are just playing church! They're playing with sacred things. We've got a lot of that going on today.

There's hope for all of us if we'll correct ourselves,

but this fellow eventually wound up on the spiritual junkheap. God had to discard his ministry because he wouldn't correct himself.

You see, when the Holy Spirit wasn't moving in spiritual gifts, this minister tried to operate spiritual gifts on his own to direct people's lives. And because that's not scriptural, he opened himself up to the devil and began hearing familiar spirits.

Familiar spirits are evil spirits that are familiar with people. They know facts about people, including believers, and those facts are often correct. They know people's names and addresses and various things about them, and they can tell what they know to those who will yield to them.

Of course, familiar spirits are not omniscient — they don't possess all knowledge, so they don't know *everything* about people. Only God is all-knowing. But familiar spirits do know some things about people. For example, they could know how much money someone has in his billfold or what he has in his pocket.

The Holy Spirit knows those things, too, and He could reveal that through the gifts of the Spirit, if He wanted to. But why would He want to? What purpose would it serve to know what someone has in his pocket? How would that glorify God? No, that's typically the work of familiar spirits.

The Holy Spirit reveals things that glorify God. For example, He could reveal a disease someone has and then heal the person! That would glorify God.

But this minister would call people out of the crowd

and tell them their name and address. Then he would
say, "I'll tell you exactly what you have in your pocket.
You've got a pen and a package of cigarettes," and then
he'd tell the congregation the brand of cigarettes.

But that wasn't the Spirit of God in operation. He
didn't minister to the person and get him delivered
from cigarette smoking by the power of the Holy Spirit!
He just wanted to draw attention to himself by display-
ing spectacular supernatural knowledge.

God knows all those things, too, and He *could* move
through a prophet like that. But He doesn't very often
demonstrate Himself like that, unless it serves a defi-
nite purpose to help someone, and it gives glory to God.

But often when familiar spirits operate through
people, many dear folks think, *Isn't that supernatural!*
And some folks do get healed because they start believing God.

I saw some ministers operate through familiar spirits in the days of *The Voice of Healing*. They could tell
you what you had in your pocket, your name, address,
and so forth. But it wasn't divinely inspired revelation.
Most of the time people who do that are operating by
familiar spirits.

A minister once called me to ask about another minister we had both known in the days of *The Voice of
Healing*. He asked me if I would recommend him. Without answering him directly, I asked, "Why are you asking me if I would recommend him?"

He answered, "I don't know. I attended one of his
services, and I didn't necessarily see anything wrong,

but there's just something that doesn't seem quite right. He says he's a prophet. He called me and wants my church to sponsor him for a meeting. But something down on the inside of me doesn't feel good about it. But I don't know why."

Without saying anything negative about the minister, I said, "Follow your spirit. Your spirit is leading you right."

I needed to say something to this pastor by way of warning him, because I knew this particular minister had caused trouble in other churches and would tear his church up spiritually too. But I didn't want to say anything critical about him, so I just confirmed what this pastor already had in his own spirit.

This so-called prophet would sometimes operate in the Holy Spirit, but then he would yield to familiar spirits and begin operating by occult powers. And before you knew it, he would be prophesying money out of people's pockets into his. Because of that, he left a bad record everywhere he preached, and he couldn't go back to any of the churches where he had ministered before.

This man's ministry was suspect by the very fact that he had to try to get someone to sponsor him for a meeting. In my ministry, I've never had to call anyone yet to be sponsored. If you leave a good record whenever you preach, people will call you for meetings, and you won't have to go around trying to get people to sponsor your meetings.

If a person's ministry is built on the Word, it will

eventually prosper. If a minister feeds the people the Word, his ministry will make a way for him. But if he tries to minister through spectacular demonstrations even when the Holy Spirit isn't moving that way, he'll get into trouble spiritually. And eventually his ministry will fail.

Sometimes there is just a fine line between fanaticism and true spirituality, and between false and genuine manifestations of spiritual gifts. Many are not able to distinguish the difference, but the Body of Christ needs to be able to do so. The Holy Spirit will always draw attention to God, and exalt the Word and the Lord Jesus Christ, not man.

Recently my wife and I went to preach for a certain group of people, and after my message, I turned to the pastor and said, "I could be wrong because I'm human; I can miss it. And sometimes it's difficult in the Spirit to distinguish between some things. But you've either been going through a terrible *physical* battle or a tremendous *spiritual* battle for the last year. If I'm wrong, just speak up and say I'm wrong."

The pastor began to cry, and said, "Brother Hagin, I've been going through a great physical battle."

I said, "Well, here's what I have in my spirit. I believe the Lord told me to tell you, 'This is the end of it. The battle is over!'"

The pastor said to me and to the congregation, "I haven't said anything to any of you about it, but fifteen years ago I had some serious physical problems. I went to some of the best doctors in America and they diagnosed it," and he gave the name of a rare disease.

"The doctors told me, 'There is nothing that can be done for you. You'll grow steadily worse and die.' But I got on top of the situation by believing God for my healing. And for fourteen years I've been all right. But last year all the symptoms came back on me. I've been in terrible pain. But, Brother Hagin, when you spoke what the Lord said — that the battle is over — all the pain left!"

I saw him at a convention a month later, and he was still completely healed and set free. That's the kind of spectacular demonstration of the gifts of the Spirit that are in line with the Word!

When it's the Holy Spirit in manifestation, people are healed and set free. And God is exalted, not a prophet.

Prophecy Taken Out of Bounds

There are so-called prophets today who teach that they can prophesy every time they lay hands on people. That's rubbish! They teach that a prophet can stand in faith to minister prophetically to people. That is not only impossible, it is unscriptural. The prophetic office is only in demonstration by the anointing of the Spirit of God, as *He* wills.

Why did Jesus appear to me more than thirty years ago tell me that He didn't put prophets in the Church to lead the Church or to guide people's lives? Because we had the same problem then as we do now. These problems just resurface with each new generation.

Now, some thirty years later, another generation has come along spiritually, and we have the same problem resurfacing today as we did then. People are taking prophecy and the prophetic office out of bounds.

For example, people write me all the time asking me to prophesy to them — even about such things as where they should go to church! Sometimes I almost feel like writing back, "If you don't have enough sense where to go to church, you're in poor spiritual condition!"

People don't need anyone to prophesy to them about where they should go to church. That's how people take the office of the prophet out of bounds scripturally and get into excess. The Bible says believers are to be led by the Spirit of God. They should know how to follow their spirit in such matters.

One man came up to me after a seminar and asked me to pray for him. He'd been going to a certain church for the last seven years, but he felt God wanted him to change churches and go back to a church he'd attended before that.

He said to me, "I want you to pray that the Lord would lead me about which church to go to."

I started to pray in agreement with him, but on the inside of me the Holy Spirit said, "Ask him what he has in his heart." So I just stopped praying, and asked him, "What is your spirit telling you? What do you have in your heart?"

He started laughing and said, "I've got to go back to

the first church." He knew all the time. God was leading him all the time. That's how we are to be led — by our *own* spirits — not by prophets!

It seems we either get in a ditch on one side of the road and back off from the prophetic office and prophecy altogether because of the excesses. Or we get in a ditch on the other side into fanaticism and extremes.

But, you see, God wants us to keep the office of the prophet and prophecy based solidly on the Word of God, just as we are to do with anything else.

Tradition tells us that the church at Thessalonica had so much prophesying that the people almost despised it. That's why Paul had to write to that church and instruct them: *"Quench not the Spirit. Despise not prophesyings. Prove all things; hold fast that which is good"* (1 Thess. 5:19-21).

God wants us to go down the middle of the road spiritually and enjoy the scriptural operation of the prophet's office and the scriptural gift of prophecy.

Be Led by the Inward Witness, Not by Prophets

When Jesus appeared to me in 1959, He emphasized that believers are to be led by the *inward witness*, not by the office of the prophet. Shortly before He appeared to me, I had been invited to hold a meeting for a certain pastor. Every time I tried to write confirming that I was coming to his church, without thinking, I'd throw away the letter. I just didn't feel good on the inside in my spirit about going to his church to preach.

But if we're not careful, we can get in the natural, reason things out, and override the inward witness. That's what I did. I got in the mental realm, and I thought, *It wouldn't hurt to go to his church. After all, I'm going to be in that area. Why travel somewhere else to preach?*

But as I kept praying for guidance about where God wanted me to preach, a certain pastor kept coming up in my spirit. He had a smaller church and had asked me to come and hold a meeting for him whenever I could.

At first I didn't pay any attention to this inward nudge of the Holy Spirit. But over a period of weeks, this pastor kept coming up in my spirit. Finally, I said to the Lord, "Surely you don't want me to go minister in his church?" But the more I thought about it, the more I had a good feeling in my spirit about it. I had a green light, so to speak, a go-ahead signal in my spirit.

The Lord appeared to me shortly after that incident in 1959 and that's when He taught me about the supernatural leading of the Holy Spirit. He said, "You couldn't go to the first church to minister because on the inside of you, in your spirit, you didn't feel good about going there. That was a stop sign, a red light, or a check in your spirit. That is the inward witness. It's not really a voice, but it's just something inside you telling you not to do that. Learn to follow that inward witness."

Jesus continued, "Now you see Me sitting here, and you hear Me talking to you. I'm telling you, 'Don't go to that church. That pastor won't accept the way you minister.' But this is the last time I'm ever going to lead you this way. I'll lead you just as I do every believer, by the inward witness.

"On the inside of you," Jesus explained, "you had an inward intuition that you were to go to another church. You discounted it, but it kept coming back to you. You see, that was the green light in your spirit that you were to go to that other church; that was the leading of the Holy Spirit. That dread you had about going to the other church was a stop sign in your spirit."

Jesus said to me in that vision, "If you'll learn to follow the inward witness, I'll make you rich. I'm not opposed to My children being rich. I'm opposed to them being covetous."

Jesus wasn't saying that every one of His children would be millionaires. To be rich means to have a full supply. Jesus was saying that He would give each one of them a full supply if they would learn to follow the inward witness — not the office of the prophet or prophecy.

Years ago, when everyone was holding tent meetings, time after time people would prophesy to me that God wanted me to get a tent. But, you see, God had never told *me* to get a tent. In fact, God had told me to stay preaching and teaching in the churches. So what these people were prophesying to me didn't line up with the leading of God in my own spirit. The Bible says we are to be led by the Holy Spirit in our own spirit — not by people prophesying to us.

So I'd just smile and say to them, "Well, when He tells me, I'll do it." I knew in my own spirit what God wanted me to do.

You see, I'm not going to run people's lives through the office of the prophet or through prophecy. And I'm not going to allow people to run my life through prophecy. You shouldn't either. I'm going to get into the Word for myself, and get ahold of God for myself. After all, I am in contact with Him, and so are you if you are a believer.

This does not mean we should be closed to sound, wise counsel in line with the Word, but our lives are not meant to be directed by other people prophesying to us.

Looking for the Spectacular And Missing the Supernatural

Too many believers are wanting someone to come along and prophesy to them and tell them what to do, when they are supposed to be led by their own spirit.

One time the Holy Spirit said to me, "My people are waiting for the spectacular and missing the supernatural." God does not often lead His people by the spectacular supernatural move of His Spirit. But the inward witness *is* supernatural because it's the Holy Ghost, and that is the number one way God leads His people.

God didn't put prophets and the gift of prophecy in the Church to guide our personal affairs. Tragedy very often happens to folks when they try to be guided by the prophet. They get their lives in a mess.

I told you about the wealthy businessman who lost everything he had because he listened to a so-called prophetess. Now I'll tell you about a businessman who never lost a penny because he learned how to listen to the inward witness — to his spirit. He wasn't led by prophecy or the office of the prophet; he was led just by the Holy Spirit in his own spirit.

I knew this man years ago. He lived in a mansion and drove expensive new cars. This was in the Depression Days. The streets were full of people out of work, but there was no work. I worked myself from sunup to sundown for one dollar and was glad to get it.

This man took ten thousand dollars in those days when money was worth more than it is today and turned it into one million dollars. He didn't do that by listening to some "prophet"! When a person was a millionaire in those days, it was like being a billionaire today.

This man said, "I've never lost a penny in any investment. People know I invest, so they come to me with their business deals. I'll listen to their projects, and many times my head will say, 'That's a good deal. You ought to get in on that.' Or someone else will come along with a deal, and my head says, 'You'd better not get in on that. You'll lose your shirt.'

"But I always say the same thing to everyone who comes to me with an investment, regardless what my head says. I always say, 'Give me two or three days to pray about it.'

"I have what I call my prayer closet. It's a closet off the master bedroom. I know God didn't mean we are literally to get into a closet to pray, but that's where I go to pray. I get in there with my Bible, and I may eat one meal a day, or I may not. I may fast. But I pray about the business deal. I ask the Lord, 'Should I or shouldn't I invest in this business deal?'"

He said, "I pray and seek the Lord until I get a yes or a no in my spirit. I spend most of the time seeking God, getting my mind quiet before God. Sometimes I have to get my mind quiet to get an answer. And sometimes it takes time to get my mind shut off; it took me time to learn how to do that. But I always get my answer within three days, sometimes in less than three days.

"Sometimes the very business deals my head said not to get involved in, my spirit also says, 'Don't do it.' Or sometimes the deal my head told me, 'You'd better not get in on that. You'll lose your shirt if you do,' my *spirit* says, 'Do it!' So I do."

He said, "I've never lost a dime in all these years." This man never consulted any prophet; he just followed the inward witness.

I was teaching in a certain place about the inward witness and what it means to be led by the Spirit, and a man came up to me after the service. He said, "Brother Hagin, if I had heard you two years ago, it would have saved me thousands upon thousands of dollars." And he went on to explain.

He told me that two years before, he'd owned all the buildings on a certain city block, which included four or five stores. Then across town, he owned another store, which was full of merchandise. All the merchandise inside the store was paid for, which included much furniture, appliances, and hardware.

He said, "I had a good cash flow and the business was in good shape financially. Then a fellow came along one day with a business deal he wanted me to invest in. I told him I'd have to pray about it. He told me that he needed his answer within three days. After that it would be too late.

"I'd heard people talk about putting out fleeces," the man said, "so I put out a fleece. According to the fleece, it looked like I should invest my money in the man's business deal, so I went to the bank and mortgaged everything I had. I put all my money in that enterprise and lost every dime of it! For the last two years I have just been paying on the interest I owe, and I still owe thousands of dollars."

He said, "If I had heard this teaching about following the inward witness, I wouldn't have lost all my money. Something on the inside of me kept telling me not to invest in his business deal, but the fleece said to do it."

Nowhere in the New Testament does it say, "As many as are led by *fleeces*, they are the sons of God."

One year at RHEMA, one of our students asked me about a fellow who was supposed to be a prophet. In the first place, if a person has to advertise to everyone he is a prophet, I wonder about his calling. In the second place, people make a mistake running around listening to every so-called prophet.

The Bible says a man's gift makes room for him

(Prov. 18:16). If a person is called to the office of the prophet, he shouldn't have to advertise it. People will know it sooner or later by the spiritual equipment that goes along with that office.

Anyway, this student said, "This prophet called me out of the crowd and prophesied over me that God had called me to Africa. He said that in so many months I'd be in Africa."

The student said, "But the thought has never entered my mind, nor have I ever had it in my spirit about going to Africa."

I asked him, "In your spirit what do you sense God wants you to do?"

He said, "I know exactly what God wants me to do. I settled all that through prayer and waiting before God."

I said, "Does it have anything to do with Africa?"

He answered, "No."

"Forget what that man told you then," I said.

"Yes, but that fellow said he was a prophet."

I said, "Just because he said he's a prophet doesn't make him one. Don't pay a bit of attention to what he said. You do what God told you in your own heart to do."

When you are grounded in the Word, you are not going to be moved by so-called prophets or their so-called prophecies. If you *are* moved by them, you are still a spiritual child tossed about with every wind of doctrine (Eph. 4:14). You need to learn to be led by the inward witness of the Holy Spirit in your spirit man.

Chapter 8
Performing in the Flesh vs. Ministering in the Spirit

We've talked about the trouble so-called prophets can get into when they try to direct people's lives through that office. Ministers can also get into trouble when they try to perform or put on something when the anointing isn't there. When ministers fall into this error, it's usually because they desire to be seen of men and to receive glory for themselves.

We had ministers get into this kind of trouble in the days of *The Voice of Healing*. In those days, there was a young man who stood in the prophetic office and was mightily used of the Holy Spirit in the word of knowledge.

I have personally seen him point to person after person in a crowd of several thousand people, and tell those he singled out exactly what was wrong with them. Each person was instantly healed. He did that under the anointing of the Holy Spirit.

But then I also saw him minister by occult powers. When the Holy Spirit wasn't moving through the gifts of the Spirit, he would try to minister supernaturally without the anointing. Because he was operating in the flesh and in the natural realm where Satan is god (2 Cor. 4:4), he opened the door for occult spirits to accommodate him.

One pastor told me that this prophet had ministered in his church too. The pastor said, "We had a woman in our church who became gravely ill, but the doctors couldn't find out what was wrong with her. Finally, she went to a specialist in New York. The specialist told her she had a rare disease and told her the name of it.

"The specialist told her, 'Only three people in the North American continent have ever had this disease and there is no cure. You'll be dead by the time you are thirty-eight.' The woman was about thirty-six years old at the time."

The pastor continued, "This prophet came to hold a meeting in my church, and the anointing of God was on him to minister in the gifts of the Spirit. He pointed to this woman in the congregation, and said, 'The doctors told you that you have a rare, incurable disease. Only three people in the North American continent have ever had this disease.' Then he spoke out the name of the disease, and said, 'The Lord has healed you.'"

The pastor told me, "This woman was instantly healed. She went back to the same doctors and they couldn't find a trace of the disease in her body.

"But," the pastor continued, "then the next night when that prophet got up to minister, the anointing wasn't there to minister by spiritual gifts, so he tried to make something happen on his own. He pointed to a woman who was the wife of one of my deacons, and said, 'The Lord shows me that you have chronic appendicitis.'"

The pastor said to me, "Everyone in the church

knew she'd never had an appendicitis problem in her life. That confused the people. I'd like to have him come back to preach because he did a lot of good. But I can't for the sake of my congregation. They don't understand how he could be right one time, and wrong another time."

The Word — A Sure Foundation

The Lord later directed me to go talk to this prophet and warn him that he was getting off in his prophetic ministry.

The Lord said to me, "You go tell him if the anointing is there to minister to people through the gifts of the Spirit, then go ahead and minister to them. If the anointing isn't there, then preach the Word. Tell him not to build his ministry on spiritual gifts, but to build it on *God's Word*. Tell him I said to develop his *preaching* ministry."

The man wasn't a teacher, but he was a preacher. The Lord said, "If he doesn't develop his preaching ministry, but keeps putting spiritual gifts first, he's going to end up on the spiritual junkheap."

What is a spiritual junkheap? Well, a junkheap is a place for discarded items. So a spiritual junkheap just means that this man's ministry would have to be discarded if he didn't change because it was hurting the Body of Christ and causing confusion.

You see, you can't build a ministry on spiritual gifts. You can't even build a ministry on a ministry office —

including the office of the prophet. And you can't build a ministry on the anointing either. In fact, you can't build a ministry on *anything* except the Word of God.

When ministers build their ministries on the Word, then the Holy Spirit can move and demonstrate Himself as He desires in spiritual gifts.

There were about one hundred and twenty ministers in *The Voice of Healing.* Many of them had marvelous spiritual gifts in operation in their lives and ministries, but they didn't have a strong foundation in the Word. I once said to some of those ministers, "When all of you fellows are gone, I'll still be out there."

They looked at me in amazement, and asked, "Why?"

I said, "Because you're building your ministries on gifts of the Spirit. I'm building my ministry on the Word of God."

Almost every one of them is gone now, but I'm still out there preaching the Word. Build your life and ministry on the Word. Put manifestations of the Spirit second. Preach and teach the Word, and let the signs follow the Word (Mark 16:17).

Anyway, I talked to this prophet for about an hour and a half, and I told him exactly what the Lord had told me to tell him. I didn't minister to him publicly. Prophets make a mistake sometimes by getting up and publicly airing everything they see and hear in the Spirit. The Holy Spirit does not embarrass or humiliate people.

This man was receptive to what I had to say, but

then he said to me, "But, Brother Hagin, people come to my meetings, and they expect me to perform."

Preachers Are *Not* Performers

I could tell he was off-course spiritually the minute he said that. I said, "You're not a performer; you're a preacher."

If a person is off-course a little bit and doesn't correct himself, eventually he'll be a lot off course! Those called to the ministry aren't *performers*! If a minister is performing, he needs to get out of the ministry.

After talking to this prophet, he began to develop his preaching ministry more. But before long, he fell right back into the same mistake. He began putting spiritual gifts first and ministering in the flesh when the anointing wasn't there.

There is a real danger in this area, because Satan operates in the realm of the flesh. So people open themselves up to the devil when they try to operate spiritual gifts in the flesh. Any minister who tries to manufacture spiritual gifts when they aren't in operation will mislead people and eventually fail because he's in error.

The next year, I was at a *Voice of Healing* convention, and this same minister was there too. The Lord spoke to me again, and said, "You go talk to him." So I went again privately and talked to him.

I said to him, "You're going to end up on the spiritual junkheap if you don't stop trying to perform and put something on for the people when the Spirit of God isn't moving. Don't try to operate in the gifts of the Spirit if you're not in the Spirit."

I told him what the Lord had told me to tell him, but I didn't know if it registered with him or not.

Shortly after that incident, I had an occasion to talk to Brother A. A. Swift, who was a missionary to China and an outstanding Bible teacher. We were discussing spiritual things, and I told him the Lord had directed me to talk to this prophet.

Brother Swift said, "I'm so glad you talked to him, Brother Hagin. He comes here every year to minister. You go to his meeting one night, and the Holy Spirit is operating through him in gifts of the Spirit. But you go the next night, and occult powers are operating through him."

Brother Swift continued, "I became acquainted with occult powers when I served as a missionary in China, so I know the difference between familiar spirits in operation and the genuine move of the Holy Spirit. But some ministers don't know the difference."

Is it possible for a person to yield to the Holy Spirit one time, and yield to evil spirits another time? Emphatically, yes! We see it in Scripture.

Peter yielded to the Holy Spirit when he said to Jesus, ". . . *Thou art the Christ, the Son of the living God*" (Matt. 16:16). Jesus said to him, ". . . *flesh and blood hath not revealed it unto thee . . .*" (Matt. 16:17). Flesh and blood didn't reveal it to Peter; the Holy Spirit revealed it to him.

As you go on reading in the same chapter, Jesus began talking about going to the Cross and dying. Peter said to Jesus, *". . . Lord: this shall not be unto thee"* (Matt. 16:22). Jesus rebuked him and said, *". . . Get thee behind me, Satan . . ."* (Matt. 16:23).

Jesus wasn't calling Peter "Satan." Jesus was just saying that Peter was yielding to Satan and speaking what Satan was saying — not what God was saying.

So Peter yielded one time to the Holy Spirit, but then he also yielded to an evil spirit. Therefore, we know from the Scriptures that it is possible to yield to the Holy Spirit one time and to an evil spirit another time.

You see, when you try to operate gifts of the Spirit yourself without the anointing, familiar spirits can accommodate you and tell you things. Paul said it this way: *"There are . . . many kinds of voices in the world, and none of them is without signification"* (1 Cor. 14:10). By operating in the flesh without the anointing, you move out into that realm where there are many spirits and many voices.

In the days of *The Voice of Healing*, for example, many good ministers missed it spiritually because they got off on a tangent, just trying to listen to what they called the "spirit," instead of listening to the Word.

Distinguishing the Voice of the Lord

A prophet better know the Voice of the Lord! Sometimes it's difficult to get young ministers to understand that every "voice" they hear is not of God. Not every voice in the spirit realm that speaks to them is the Holy Spirit.

I don't say that to make people fearful. But on the other hand, it is better to be cautious and be safe than to be sorry. And if a prophet, or any believer for that matter, doesn't know the Voice of the Lord, he shouldn't act on what he hears until he knows! It's better to do nothing than to act hastily on what a person *thinks* is the Lord.

Sometimes nothing but growth and grace will teach believers some of these things. Ministers shouldn't be afraid, but they *should* be cautious. And they shouldn't go around saying, "Thus saith the Lord" about every voice they hear in the spirit realm either.

Early in my ministry, I said to the Lord, "Lord, I'm not acting on any voice I hear until I know the difference between the Voice of the Holy Spirit and the voice of evil spirits."

Of course, the Lord trains us by His Spirit as we study and meditate in the Word. As God's Word abides in us, we begin to learn how to distinguish between the different voices in the spirit realm, and we get to know the Voice of the Holy Spirit. The Voice of the Holy Spirit always lines up with the Word of God (John 16:13,15; 1 John 5:8).

When I was young in ministry, at times I was sure the Holy Spirit had spoken to me, but when I acted on what He said, nothing happened; there weren't any results. For example, sometimes in a meeting when the Holy Spirit gave me a word of knowledge for someone, and I spoke that out to the congregation, no one responded. It caused me to doubt whether the Holy Spirit had really spoken to me.

Or sometimes I was directed by the Holy Spirit to give an altar call, or to call out a particular healing and no one responded. The Voice of the Holy Spirit was just as real to me as though a person were talking right next to me. But no one in the congregation responded.

Other times when I spoke out what the Holy Spirit gave me, those in the congregation responded, and wonderful things happened as a result of obeying the promptings of the Holy Spirit.

The Lord explained this to me. He said, "There are two things that are involved when this happens. First of all, the people in the congregation have something to do with it; they have a responsibility to respond to the Holy Spirit too.

"Many times you've heard the Voice of the Holy Spirit correctly, but people also have their part to play. They needed to respond to what the Holy Spirit said through you, the minister."

The minister may hear God correctly, but people still have free will, and they can choose whether or not they will respond to God.

"Then, secondly," Jesus explained, "there is an evil spirit whose voice sounds very similar to the Voice of the Holy Spirit. That voice is very similar to the voice of prophecy, except that it magnifies and lifts up man, not God."

Of course, the genuine spirit of prophecy is the Voice of the Holy Spirit (Rev. 19:10).

You see, there are many spirits and many voices in the spirit realm (1 Cor. 14:10). Jesus said, "Nearly every minister — and every believer — as he is maturing spiritually, sometimes listens unknowingly to that other voice. He hasn't yet learned to distinguish between it and the Holy Spirit. That's another reason nothing happens or the wrong thing happens when they minister."

Does that mean a believer has a demon when he listens to the wrong voice? No, of course not. No more than Peter had a devil when he yielded to Satan and reported what Satan said (Matt. 16:21-23). James and John also yielded to the wrong spiritual influence (Luke 9:54-56) and were rebuked by Jesus.

You see, spiritual things — both the Word of God and spirit voices — have to be rightly divided. People can listen to the wrong voice just as they can wrongly "divide" or misinterpret the Scriptures.

Believers don't need to be fearful of following the wrong voice as long as they stay in the Word. But that's why they must line up everything they hear with the Word of God, because the Spirit and the Word agree (1 John 5:8).

Also, the Bible promises that the Holy Spirit will lead us into all truth (John 16:13). Jesus Himself said, ". . . [His] *sheep follow him: for they know his voice. And a stranger will they not follow, but will flee from him:*

for they know not the voice of strangers" (John 10:4,5).

Therefore, if you hear something in the spirit realm that is contrary to the Word of God, you would know *not* to follow that.

As every minister and every believer is growing up spiritually, he will have to learn to distinguish between these two voices. As Jesus said to me, sometimes nothing but growth and grace — time and experience in the Word and in the Spirit — will teach a person some of these things.

Sometimes people desire to be used by God so much that they move out in the realm of the spirit and try to do something themselves in the natural realm where Satan is god (2 Cor. 4:4). And then these spirits come in and accommodate them. Those who do this go into error, because they are trying to call attention to themselves, instead of bringing glory to God.

It's better just to wait and be sure it is the Holy Spirit talking to you. If you're not sure, don't move out on what you hear in the spirit.

I know in my own ministry when the Holy Spirit is moving, and I'm not exactly sure what God wants me to do, I just wait on God to direct me. If I can't get clear in my spirit what He wants me to do, I just keep quiet and go ahead and preach the Word. The Word always works because it's anointed.

What will keep you from getting off and listening to voices other than the Holy Spirit? Stay close to God. Stay in the Word. Desire to exalt and lift up God and His Word, not yourself.

Years ago I saw some fellows get off spiritually, whom God no doubt had called and used at one time in the prophetic ministry. But I noticed that before their meetings, these fellows didn't spend their time study- ing, praying, or seeking God. They ran around all day long cracking jokes and visiting with people.

But it always amazed me that then later when they got up to minister in their services, the "gift" still oper- ated through them. I came to understand that they weren't operating in the gifts of the Holy Spirit — it was the work of familiar spirits.

I know from experience that when I'm holding a meeting, I can't run around all day long and then expect to get up in the service and operate under the anointing!

The Holy Spirit has always emphasized to me when I'm holding meetings, "Stay away from people. Wait before Me in prayer and in the Word." I've made that a practice over the years. As I am faithful to do that, spir- itual gifts operate in a greater measure in my ministry.

But when you can run around all day long, neglect- ing the Word and prayer, and then just get up and auto- matically operate "in the Spirit," something is wrong!

Correct Operation of Spiritual Gifts

It's so important for prophets to make sure they stay within scriptural boundaries in the operation of spiritual gifts in their lives and ministries.

Actually, there is no instruction given about how the

gifts of the Spirit operate except for the utterance gifts. But there is a reason the Bible gives us instruction and warning about the proper use of the *utterance* gifts of the Holy Spirit — tongues, interpretation of tongues, and prophecy.

You see, believers have something to do with the manifestation of these gifts. We do the speaking, but the Holy Ghost gives the utterance. We have to *yield* to the promptings of the Holy Spirit and speak out in faith what God has given us.

Even though the utterance gift is perfect, the manifestation through the believer is not always perfect. Think about it. Believers can prophesy, speak in tongues, and interpret *at will*, even though it may not be prompted by the Holy Spirit. They could do those things entirely in the flesh, imitating the Holy Spirit.

That's why there must be scriptural guidelines governing the operation of the utterance gifts. The believer has a part to play in cooperating with the Holy Spirit.

Notice that the Bible doesn't say anything about how the revelation gifts and the power gifts operate: the word of knowledge, word of wisdom, discerning of spirits; gifts of healings, special faith, or the working of miracles.

Yes, the believer still has to cooperate and yield to the Holy Spirit and obey His promptings in the operation of these gifts too. However, on the other hand, the believer can't give himself a miracle, produce a vision, or heal anyone.

In that sense, the believer himself has nothing to do

with the operation of those gifts. Either the Holy Spirit works a miracle, or He doesn't; you can't make a miracle happen. Either you have a bona-fide revelation of the Holy Spirit, or you don't. You could dream up something and imagine God said something to you, but it won't come to pass.

In that sense, the believer doesn't have anything to do with the operation of the revelation and power gifts. But in the utterance gifts, the believer works in cooperation with the Holy Spirit.

That is why the Bible says the utterance gifts, operating as they do in dependence upon the believer, need to be judged (1 Cor. 14:29). Some prophecies are easy to judge. For example, it was easy to judge the prophecy a woman once gave in church: "My little children, if you are my little children, don't be afeard. But if you are afeard, I don't blame you. Sometimes I get afeard myself."

I notice in the Word that every time God came on the scene, He said, "Fear not." So that prophecy was easy to judge because it didn't line up with the Word of God. But there are some times that prophecy is not so easy to judge.

On one hand, we don't want to be on the defensive in the area of prophetic utterance, suspicious of everyone and every utterance. But on the other hand, we don't want to be like young mockingbirds either, who open their mouths wide, allowing anything to be poked down their throats.

Believers need to realize that the gifts of the Spirit

and the Holy Ghost are *perfect*, but human beings are *imperfect*. The Holy Ghost manifests Himself through imperfect vessels, so the manifestation through a person is not always perfect.

That's why prophets particularly need to make sure they stay within scriptural guidelines in their ministries, because they operate more consistently in utterance gifts of the Spirit than any other ministry gift.

The Balance Between the Word and the Spirit

Every prophet needs to be solidly rooted in the Word, or it will be too easy for him to get off trying to follow after the "Spirit," and depart from the Word. Actually, every believer, and certainly those called to the fivefold ministry, need a balance in their spiritual walk between the Word and the Holy Spirit.

In my ministry, for example, along with the prophetic gift, I also have a teaching gift. That has brought balance to my ministry. I know from experience that if a prophet is not in the Word, he can tend to try to follow too much after the "Spirit," and he can get things in a mess. But if he is solid in the Word, the Word will keep him steady.

I've also seen a balance or blend in other ministries too. For example, I've seen husband and wife ministry teams in which one was a prophet and the other had a solid teaching ministry. The one would help balance the other one spiritually. The two ministry gifts working together provided a good combination of ministries and a solid spiritual balance.

One couple in particular was well-balanced ministe-
rially. The wife was no doubt a prophetess, and her husband was a pastor and a teacher. The spectacular
spiritual gifts manifested through the wife's prophetic
ministry in the church. But her husband's solid teaching ministry steadied her and gave balance to her ministry. A blend of these ministries can be a great asset in
the ministry and mightily used by God.

Also, if one is called to more than one office, he will
need to understand which ministry has the priority. For
example, I got into trouble with the Lord when I left off
my prophetic ministry to some extent and put my
teaching ministry first.

I stepped back from the prophetic ministry some-
what because at that time there were those who called
themselves prophets, but were creating all kinds of
havoc in the Body of Christ. I didn't want to be classed
with the false, so I stepped back prophetically. When I
did that, I got into trouble, and the Lord had to correct
me.

One minister in particular caused a great deal of
confusion in the days of *The Voice of Healing*, particularly in the deliverance ministry. At one time he was
marvelously used of God in spiritual gifts. I saw God do
some of the greatest miracles I've ever seen in my life
through this man's ministry. But he got off into
excesses, and it ruined his ministry and eventually cost
him his life.

You see, eventually a prophet or any minister will
lose the anointing if he's not walking in the light of the

Word. In the natural, if you get a freight train going full speed and let it run out of fuel, for a while, it will still keep going.

In the same way, some prophets have run out of the anointing and power of the Holy Spirit because their ministries aren't based solidly on the Word to give them spiritual fuel. Yet for a while they still keep going.

Many folks can't tell when a minister is preaching without the anointing. But just because a prophet can preach, doesn't mean he's preaching under the anointing. Many people don't know the difference between *inspiration* and *perspiration*! Just because a minister is a fast talker, doesn't mean he's inspired by the Holy Spirit.

Don't Pervert the Gift of God

Staying teachable and staying in the Word will help keep a person from getting off spiritually. I don't know about you, but I've always made it a practice to listen to others who have wisdom and knowledge in the Word.

Even when I was a young minister, I listened to older men of God who had been down the road spiritually before me. These were men who had years of ministerial experience and knew the Spirit of God. The things they shared with me helped me immeasurably in many areas.

One area where the Body of Christ needs some wisdom from experienced ministers is in understanding that there are religious cons in the ministry. Some of these religious cons call themselves prophets. For example, some ministers who were at one time used by God in revelation gifts, particularly the word of knowledge, have perverted those gifts.

It seems whenever they have a word of knowledge, it's always about money. For example, I heard one so-called prophet say, "There is a woman who has $10,000. If she will send it to me, God will save her husband."

Well, there's bound to be some dear woman with an unsaved husband who will send him that money. But any minister who uses spiritual gifts to prophesy money into his ministry is a *false* prophet! A person like that isn't in the Spirit — he's just learned how to maneuver and manipulate people. He's money-minded, and he's lost the anointing of the Holy Spirit.

Many who have perverted spiritual gifts were no doubt at one time used by God. But the anointing on their ministries lifted when they got so money-minded that they perverted the gift of God for personal gain. And when a minister is no longer teachable and open to the correction of others, he is in bad shape spiritually.

There was a man in the days of *The Voice of Healing* whom God used mightily. I once saw him point to a man in the congregation and say, "God shows me that you have a rupture."

He told the man how many years he'd had the rupture. Then he prayed for the man, and the rupture disappeared instantly. The man who was healed was a successful businessman. He was thrilled to be healed because he had suffered greatly.

Several years after this businessman had been healed, he asked me, "Do you think that prophet was right on spiritually?"

I asked, "Why?"

He said, "Well, I was healed, all right. But every time that minister saw me after that, he prophesied money out of me."

Finally after two or three years, this businessman caught on. He should have caught on the first time. Anyone prophesying money out of your pocket into theirs is wrong. Never accept the ministry of someone who is always prophesying money out of people!

A prophet should never use spiritual gifts for personal gain. Some ministers tell you to plant your money into their ministries as a seed faith for your healing. But they are walking on dangerous ground. Healing belongs to you even if you don't have a dime!

Ministers need to be careful, particularly where money is concerned. Some ministers just want your financial support, and they try to obtain it by questionable means. They aren't necessarily concerned first and foremost about ministering to people or being a blessing to them. Ministers of the gospel should be in the ministry to help and bless people, not for personal gain.

But, you see, just because any minister, including a prophet, produces fruit in his ministry, doesn't mean his life or ministry is one hundred percent right on with God.

Christians shouldn't be skeptical of ministers of the gospel. On the other hand, there are spiritual cons in the ministry who have perverted the gift of God; they are motivated by personal gain.

So Christians can't always just look at the fruit a minister produces publicly to determine if his ministry is right on spiritually. Does he walk uprightly before God? Does his life reflect the gravity of his high call to the ministry? Are spiritual gifts used according to scriptural guidelines? These are questions which will help the Body of Christ from being taken in by charlatans in the ministry.

True Manifestations of Revelation Gifts

Occasionally, the Holy Spirit will reveal certain facts about people to a prophet. But it is usually not to be told to others. The prophet needs to be careful not to draw attention to himself or to embarrass others publicly by what he knows in the Spirit.

For example, one time I walked into one of our fellowship meetings years ago, and I saw a fellow I'd never seen before. I said to myself, *I wonder who that is?* On the inside of me the Holy Spirit said, "That's So-and-so. He goes to the First Assembly, and he lives at such-and-such a place."

I never told anyone that the Holy Spirit revealed all that to me; I didn't want to attract attention to myself. The Holy Spirit told me that for a reason, but it wasn't so I could broadcast it and show everyone how "spiritual" I was.

So on rare occasions, a prophet may know certain

facts about a person through the word of knowledge, but usually he isn't to tell anyone else about it. There may be a legitimate use of the word of knowledge along this line if the prophet isn't using it to extort money out of people. Often the word of knowledge stimulates people's faith and helps them believe God for themselves.

There is a true manifestation of the revelation gifts in the prophet's ministry. But sometimes prophets who are called and equipped by God, think, *I am obligated to perform*. When the Holy Spirit isn't in manifestation, they try to operate spiritual gifts. But they're in the flesh, and that's a dangerous place to be in.

To stay on course in his life and ministry, a prophet must always make sure he is basing his ministry on the Word and not on spiritual gifts. For the prophet, and every other fivefold ministry gift, the Word of God is the *only* sure foundation.

Chapter 9
Foretelling vs. Forthtelling

In a previous chapter, we saw that one difference between Old and New Testament prophets is that New Testament prophets don't guide or direct believers. In the 1959 visitation, Jesus also talked to me about another difference between Old and New Testament prophets.

Jesus said, "The office of the prophet in the Old Testament consisted more of *foretelling*, whereas the office of the prophet under the New Covenant consists more of *forthtelling*. However, God may occasionally use New Testament prophets to foretell future events, too, through the word of wisdom.

Under the Old Covenant, a major part of the prophet's ministry had to do with *foretelling*. Many times the prophets of the Old Testament would preach to the people and then begin to prophesy, foretelling about the coming Messiah. Then they would take right up where they had left off, preaching inspirationally to the Israelites about following God.

Some people think a major part of the prophet's ministry under the New Testament is also to foretell future events. However, that is not the main part of his ministry, although that could manifest occasionally as the Spirit of God wills.

Diversities of Anointing

It's important to understand that in each ministry gift there are diversities of anointings. For example, as I said, some prophets minister more in the *preaching* anointing. Other prophets minister more in the *teaching* anointing.

Also, some New Testament prophets were not used in the word of wisdom at all. In other words, they did not foretell anything; they were more *preaching* prophets as was John the Baptist.

John's prophetic ministry consisted of preaching repentance and baptizing folks. We have no record in the Bible that he predicted or foretold any future events except: "*. . . There cometh one mightier than I after me, the latchet of whose shoes I am not worthy to stoop down and unloose*" (Mark 1:7).

The Bible also says that Judas and Silas were prophets, but we see no foretelling in their ministries either. The Bible doesn't record that they gave anyone personal messages either. The Bible says Judas and Silas "*. . . exhorted the brethren with many words, and confirmed them*" (Acts 15:32). In other words, Judas and Silas preached the Word to the people and encouraged them in the ways of the Lord.

On the other hand, some prophets were used in the word of wisdom, as was Agabus. By this we can see the diversities of anointings even within the prophetic office.

You realize, of course, that it is the word of wisdom operating in the prophet's ministry that enables him to foretell future events because it brings a revelation about an event that will occur in the future, or about the plans and purposes of God.

However, the word of wisdom manifests *only as the Spirit wills.* And even though a prophet's predictions come to pass, the final proof that he is a prophet is that his prophecies line up with the Word of God (Deut. 13:1-5).

But the main emphasis of the prophet's ministry in the New Testament is on *forthtelling* — preaching or teaching the Word by inspired utterance. Even under the Old Covenant, the prophets didn't always prophesy about the future. That was manifested, of course, but they were mainly preachers — prophet preachers.

Actually, if you'll read about the prophets of the Old Testament, you'll find that the prophets' *public* ministry consisted mostly of preaching. In fact, many of the supernatural manifestations in their ministries occurred privately on an individual basis, not to an entire group or congregation of people.

We find an example of the prophet's ministry in demonstration *privately* in Elijah's ministry, as he ministered to the widow woman at Zarephath (1 Kings 17:9-16). The cruse of oil and the meal barrel just kept miraculously pouring out oil and meal (1 Kings 17:14). That miracle was done privately in the widow's house.

When Naaman was healed of leprosy, it wasn't done in a public service. Elisha didn't even go out to see Naaman. He just sent his servant out to speak the word of the Lord to Naaman: ". . . *Go and wash in Jordan seven times, and thy flesh shall come again to thee, and thou shalt be clean"* (2 Kings 5:10). Naaman was healed, but it wasn't done publicly.

Naaman was so grateful to be healed, he wanted to give Elisha gifts of silver and gold and changes of raiment. Elisha refused to receive them. He had enough sense to know when to take gifts and when not to; he wasn't money-minded.

But Elisha's servant, Gehazi, ran after Naaman, lied to him, and received the gifts. Naaman was so thrilled to be healed of an incurable disease, he gave Gehazi twice as much as he asked for. But by a word of knowledge, Elisha found out about it and pronounced the judgment of the Lord on Gehazi — the leprosy of Naaman.

All that was done privately, not publicly (2 Kings 5:25-27). Elisha was in his own house; he didn't do that before a congregation of people.

Prophets Don't Know Everything

There's something else in this passage I want you to see about the prophet. Prophets don't know everything; they only know what God reveals to them.

For example, Gehazi would not have followed after Naaman if he'd thought Elisha knew everything. If Elisha knew everything through spiritual gifts, Gehazi wouldn't have been so foolish as to take silver and clothes from Naaman.

Sometimes people have thought that because I am a

prophet, I have unlimited knowledge about them. For instance, they've thought I could give them a word from the Lord any time I wanted to. People have even called me all hours of the day and night, seeking a "word" from the Lord. But people need to realize that the prophet can't turn spiritual gifts on and off as he wants to.

The Word of Knowledge Operating *Privately* In the Prophet's Ministry

We can see an example of the word of knowledge operating *privately* in a prophet's ministry in this passage in Second Kings. Elisha said to Gehazi, ". . . *Went not mine heart with thee, when the man turned again from his chariot to meet thee? . . .*" (2 Kings 5:26). Elisha was alone in his house when the word of knowledge occurred.

This was a word of knowledge because it revealed a certain fact known to God — that Gehazi took silver and clothes from Naaman. It came through the gift of discerning of spirits because Elisha saw this in the realm of the spirit.

That's what Elisha meant when he said, "My spirit went with you when you joined yourself to Naaman's chariot, and I saw what you did." Elisha was a seer; he saw into the realm of the spirit when his spirit went with Gehazi. But even then, these spiritual gifts were in operation privately. Also, Elisha confronted Gehazi privately.

Several times in my ministry, I've had experiences

similar to Elisha's. The gift of discerning of spirits operated in conjunction with the word of knowledge. Very often spiritual gifts work together.

For example, sometimes I've gotten up to preach, and suddenly in the Spirit, I was in another place. Physically I was still preaching in that pulpit. But in the Spirit, the Lord took me to another place because He had something to show me.

For example, one time in the middle of a sermon, the Lord took me by His Spirit to another part of town. I was standing on a street corner miles away. I knew it was the night before. It was the word of knowledge in operation, because it was a fragment of God's omniscient knowledge concerning something in the past.

I saw one of my church members, a young woman, walking down the street, and in the Spirit, I saw a man drive up in a car. This young woman got into the car, and suddenly in the Spirit it was as if I was in the backseat. The couple drove out into the country and committed adultery.

My spirit went with them, just as Elisha's spirit went with Gehazi when Elisha said, ". . . *Went not mine heart* [spirit] *with thee . . . ?*" (2 Kings 5:26). God showed me that to protect me. I was single at the time, and several church members had been trying to get me to date this young woman.

The word of knowledge working in conjunction with the discerning of spirits has occurred in my ministry more than once. Many times when I have experienced this operation of the word of knowledge, it has been on a private basis.

You ask, "Is that a scriptural experience?" Absolutely, as we see here in Second Kings. In the world, people have spiritual experiences they call "out-of-the-body" experiences. That has no relation to what I'm talking about at all. That experience is a perversion of genuine gifts of the Spirit in operation.

The operation of spiritual gifts — the word of knowledge and the discerning of spirits — is something that happens by the power of the Holy Spirit. Just because the devil can do some things doesn't negate the genuine move of the Holy Spirit. Just stay with the Word. God can top anything the devil is doing.

Much of the time the miracles God performed through the Old Testament prophets were done on a one-to-one basis. Once in a while God did use the prophets publicly, as in the case of Elijah with the prophets of Baal (1 Kings 18:17-40).

You see, in some respects we've had a distorted view of the prophetic office. And some folks think when there is not a public display of manifestations of the Spirit all the time in the prophet's office, that means they are not in operation. But many times they are in operation privately every day in his ministry, but he just doesn't tell it publicly.

Look at Jesus' ministry to the woman at the well. That was a private encounter. He confronted her privately by a word of knowledge when He said, ". . . *thou hast had five husbands; and he whom thou now hast is not thy husband: in that saidst thou truly*" (John 4:18).

You see, the prophet's ministry doesn't only take place in the pulpit. In fact, it probably occurs with more frequency privately and in one-to-one encounters with people.

Let me give you an example of the word of knowledge operating *publicly* in my ministry. Very often the word of knowledge can be used in the prophet's ministry to bring a sinner to repentance, as in Jesus' ministry to the woman at the well.

I was holding a meeting in Texas, and as I gave the altar call, suddenly the Spirit of God came upon me. There was a tall fellow standing in the back of the church, and the Holy Spirit told me to minister to him prophetically.

I asked him to stand out in the aisle. I had no idea what I was going to do or what I was going to say. If the anointing of the Holy Spirit had lifted right then, I would have been sunk. I had no idea what to say to him.

But then under the inspiration of the Spirit, I found myself saying these words: "Well, I'm going to go tonight, but I want you to know that I don't believe in that fellow preaching down there. He's nothing but a fake — laying hands on people and getting them to fall down! He's just hypnotizing people; that's what he's doing! I'm just going to please you, and that's the only reason I'm going! I don't believe in all that!"

Then I said to this man, "You said those words to your wife before you came to church tonight."

Then under the unction of the Holy Spirit, I began to quote other words he had said, and as I was speak-

ing, that man ran down the aisle and slid into the altar!
He must have gotten saved running down the aisle,
because when he slid into the altar, he was speaking in
tongues!

But I want to you to notice something about the
scriptural use of the word of knowledge in the prophet's
office. This word of knowledge was to bring a sinner to
repentance — it was to God's glory. It had nothing to do
with anything as inconsequential as what someone had
in his pocket!

However, the prophet's main ministry in public is
still to preach or teach the Word of God to people under
the inspiration of the Holy Spirit. That's true for both
Old and New Testament prophets.

The Word of Wisdom in the Prophet's Ministry

In the New Testament, we do have two scriptural
examples of the word of wisdom operating in a
prophet's ministry as he foretold future events. These
examples occurred in the ministry of Agabus.

> **ACTS 11:28**
> **28 And there stood up one of them named Agabus,
> and signified by the spirit that there should be
> great dearth [drought] throughout all the world:
> which came to pass in the days of Claudius Cae-
> sar.**

In Acts 11, Agabus prophesied about a drought that
was coming. His revelation accurately predicted a
future event, but it didn't lay any additional doctrine of
the New Testament. Agabus wasn't in the same class as

the foundational prophets.

Also, the word that Agabus brought did not provide direction or guidance to the Church, except to prepare believers for what was ahead. He wasn't prophesying about which doctrines should be preached or that people should submit to his ministry.

Acts 21 also shows Agabus standing in the office of the prophet as foreteller.

> **ACTS 21:10,11**
> **10 And as we tarried there** [in Jerusalem] **many days, there came down from Judaea a certain prophet, named Agabus.**
> **11 And when he was come unto us, he took Paul's girdle, and bound his own hands and feet, and said, Thus saith the Holy Ghost, So shall the Jews at Jerusalem bind the man that owneth this girdle, and shall deliver him into the hands of the Gentiles.**

Agabus gave forth a word of wisdom which he received from the Holy Ghost. He told Paul what would happen to him in Jerusalem. We don't really know that Agabus brought forth this word of wisdom to Paul *spontaneously* through the vehicle of prophecy. By using the expression, "Thus saith the Holy Ghost," Agabus may just have been reporting what the Holy Ghost had already said to him previously.

Through the office of the prophet, God sometimes tells people what is about to take place to help prepare them for things that are ahead. But notice that Agabus was not telling Paul whether or not to go to Jerusalem.

In other words, Agabus was not giving Paul guid-

ance or direction about what Paul should do. Agabus
was only reporting what was awaiting Paul if he did go
to Jerusalem. Paul had to make his own decision about
going to Jerusalem.

Actually, the Holy Spirit just witnessed or confirmed
what would happen if Paul went to Jerusalem. We
notice in Acts 20:22,23 that Paul seemed to have
already been made aware of this personally by the Holy
Spirit. In my own prophetic ministry, I tell people all
the time that any personal prophecy that comes
through me must bear witness with their own spirit.

The Private and Public Operation
Of the Word of Wisdom

In my ministry as a prophet, God has sometimes
used me to foretell certain future events through the
word of wisdom — many times privately and occasionally publicly.

However, my main ministry as a prophet is to
preach and teach the Word of God. As the Spirit wills,
these other manifestations occur. But I never seek a
vision or seek to hear anything from the Lord; these
supernatural manifestations occur spontaneously as
the Holy Spirit wills.

The Revelation Gifts
In Operation *Privately* To Warn People

There are times God will reveal to a prophet something that is going to happen so the prophet can warn

the people involved. For example, in the days of *The Voice of Healing*, I went to see a minister who had a large tent that seated thousands. A large crowd like that was almost unheard of in those days.

The minister showed me his tent, and when we finished talking, I went to get into my car. As I did, the Spirit of God said to me, "Go tell him he's not going to live much longer unless he judges himself in three areas. Number one, on money."

This man had used the manifestation of spiritual gifts in his ministry to raise money. That's not only *not* scriptural; it's not ethical. Those who are called to the ministry, including prophets, need to be very careful about money. Ministers shouldn't be out for money. Folks can't use the ministry to raise money for themselves. Some folks in our day are flirting with disaster in this area and are right on the edge of it.

Then the Lord said to me, "Number two, tell him that he needs to judge himself on love. He's not walking in love toward his fellow ministers." This man would cut down fellow ministers without hesitation if they happened to cross him.

Then Jesus said, "Number three, tell him to judge himself on his diet." This minister didn't seem to exercise any self-control in his eating habits.

Here again, this was a private manifestation of gifts of the Spirit operating in the office of the prophet. Probably ninety percent of the time, the prophet's ministry is in demonstration privately. Sometimes the Lord will instruct a prophet to go tell the person what the Lord has shown him, and sometimes He won't.

This time the Lord told me to go tell the man what the Lord had said. I started to get out of my car to go talk to the man, but just then someone else began talking to him. I sat back down in my car, and then my human reasoning took over.

I began to think, *He's not going to listen to me anyway.* As I sat there reasoning to myself, the minister I was supposed to talk to got in his car and drove away. I never had another opportunity to tell him what the Lord had shown me.

About three and a half years later, I was at a *Voice of Healing* convention. Word came that this minister was dying. Brother Lindsay invited all the ministers who were present to come up on the platform and agree together in prayer for this man's healing.

I started to walk up to the platform, but the Spirit of God said to me, "Don't go up there."

I stopped dead still, and asked, "Why not?"

He said, "Because he's going to die."

I asked, "Why is he going to die?"

The Holy Spirit said, "Because he wouldn't judge himself and walk in love towards his fellow ministers. I judged him, and turned him over to Satan for the destruction of the flesh, that his spirit may be saved in the day of the Lord Jesus" (1 Cor. 5:5).

So I just turned around and went to the back of the auditorium. Later that minister died just as the Lord had said he would.

Another instance of private foretelling occurred in my ministry in January 1964. Several of us had gone to a restaurant. We were sitting at the table getting ready to order, when the Spirit of the Lord came upon me. I said to one of our board members who was there, "I've got to pray, and I've got to pray now."

We got up and left and went to my hotel room and began praying. And then the word of wisdom began to operate through prophecy. I prophesied for two hours. I've never had an anointing quite like that. It seemed like there were two of me, as I sat there listening to myself prophesy.

In all these years of ministry, an experience like this one has only happened twice. You see, these things occur as the Spirit wills. In that prophecy in the hotel room, the Lord took us through six years and told us about things to come. He told us what would happen in Vietnam and some things that would happen in our government.

In this prophecy, the Lord also said, "At the end of '65, he who now stands in the forefront of the healing ministry as a prophet will be taken out of the way. He'll make a false step and Satan shall destroy his life, but his spirit will be saved, and his works will follow him. Ere '66 shall come, he shall be gone."

I took that prophecy to Brother Lindsay, because it's scriptural to have other spiritual men judge prophecy. I never made it public. Prophets make a mistake by publicly broadcasting some of these things.

On December 27, 1965, my wife was at the beauty

parlor, and she called home to say that this minister, who was the leading prophet at the time, had been in an automobile accident. He was unconscious, and doctors said he would never regain consciousness.

I told her, "There is no use praying. He'll be dead within two or three days." I said that because I remembered what the Lord had said in that prophecy. Then the Lord explained to me, "I had to permit him to be removed because of the damage he was causing in the Body of Christ."

Two days later, Brother Lindsay called me and said, "Brother Hagin, the brother you referred to just died. I got out that prophecy the Lord gave us eighteen months ago and read it. It's right on."

Brother Lindsay related an experience he'd had with that prophet. Brother Lindsay said, "I told him, 'You're not a teacher, so don't try to teach.'" He was a preacher and a good one at that, and he had marvelous manifestations of the Holy Spirit in his ministry.

Brother Lindsay said, "I begged him not to teach. I said, 'You don't know the Bible, and you're confusing folks. Leave the Bible teaching to the teachers. Just go ahead and preach and exercise the word of knowledge and gifts of healings as the Spirit wills, and be a blessing to the Body of Christ.'"

This prophet said to Brother Lindsay, "I know I'm not a teacher, but I want to teach. And I'm going to teach!"

It's dangerous to intrude into a ministry office to which you are not called. In the Old Testament, if people intruded into a holy place that was reserved for those who held certain offices, they instantly fell dead. Under grace, people in disobedience can last for a while. But sooner or later, those who intrude into ministry offices to which they are not called will be judged.

Many times folks see someone minister in the prophet's office, and they say, "I prophesy, so I can stand in the office of the prophet too." But they can't. If they'll keep the gift of prophecy in the realm where it should be — simple prophecy unto edification, exhortation, and comfort — they will be fine. If not, they will get into trouble.

It is dangerous to intrude into another man's office. And, really, the Body of Christ has not had the respect and reverence for ministries, gifts, and manifestations of the Spirit we ought to have. We treat the things of God too lightly.

Then Brother Lindsay related something else to me that had happened regarding this same prophet. He said to me, "This past year, I was praying with my wife and Sister Schrader about the work of the ministry. (Sister Schrader was a prophetess who has since gone on to be with the Lord.)

"We were praying about different projects in our ministry. Right in the middle of the prayer, Sister Schrader blurted out, 'Go warn Brother _____ (and called this minister's name)! He's going to die.'"

Brother Lindsay said, "I was busy, and I let that get by me, and I didn't go warn him like I was supposed to. Then later, my wife and I and Sister Schrader were again praying about ministry projects. Again Sister Schrader blurted out right in the middle of prayer, 'Go warn Brother _____ (and called this minister's name). He's going to die. He's walking in the way of Dowie.'"

Here's something about the office of the prophet I want to get across to you. Sometimes when a prophet speaks by the unction of the Spirit, it can seem illogical. It may seem to interrupt what is going on because it comes spontaneously from the Holy Spirit.

In other words, when Sister Schrader blurted this out about this prophet, it had no relation to what they were praying about at all. It didn't seem to fit with what was going on, but the Holy Spirit had something He wanted to get over to them.

Brother Lindsay said, "I called around to see if I could locate this minister, and I finally found where he was holding a meeting. I called him and talked to him personally. I told him, 'I have something important to talk to you about. I want to fly out and talk to you in person. Will you be there?'"

The minister assured Brother Lindsay, saying, "Yes, I'll be here three days."

Brother Lindsay told me, "I flew out there, and when I got there, he was gone. Some fellows had come along and wanted him to go hunting with them back up in the mountains. So he went with them and wouldn't be back for three days. I couldn't sit there and wait on him for three days, so I had to leave."

Brother Lindsay said, "Later that same year, my wife and I and Sister Schrader were praying again, and

Sister Schrader suddenly blurted out about the same prophet, 'Go warn Brother _____ (and called this minister's name)! He's walking in the way of Dowie. He's going to die. Go now!'

"So I checked around and found out where he was holding a meeting and found out that he would be there several days. I flew to the nearest city, rented a car, and drove to the town where he was preaching.

"After his morning meeting," Brother Lindsay said, "I talked to him as the Lord had instructed me, but I saw that he wouldn't listen. I said to myself, *Well, he'll just have to die then.* And not too long after that, he did die."

That's unfortunate, and it's not God's best. But it happens sometimes when people in the ministry won't judge themselves, and they aren't teachable.

When God told me to go talk to that minister I mentioned, and tell him he was going to die unless he judged himself — he could have changed it if he had judged himself. He didn't have to die, if only he had judged the sin in his life. Sometimes things can be changed; sometimes they can't. God knows.

Here's another thing. There is a principle involved here. Be careful who you follow after spiritually. What did that prophecy mean, "He's walking in the way of Dowie"? Sister Schrader didn't even know what that meant; she didn't know Dowie.

This prophet had proclaimed that he was Elijah that was to come, and that he was the messenger of the covenant. But Jesus is the Messenger of the Covenant!

Dowie had proclaimed the same thing. I read one of Dowie's sermons in which he proclaimed, "I'm Elijah number three." This prophet who died also said he was Elijah. That's what the Lord meant by, "He's walking in the way of Dowie."

Be careful who you read after. Be careful who you follow after spiritually. Make sure you are following ministers of the gospel only as they follow Christ. Be sure they are rooted and grounded in the Word of God.

I could give you other examples of those who went into the same doctrinal error as the one they studied extensively after. They took upon themselves the same type of ministry, or the same spirit, so to speak, as that other person.

That can be good or bad depending on which spirit the minister yielded to — the Holy Spirit or evil spirits.

Some way or another, whoever you follow after spiritually, or study after extensively, the "anointing" on that person will become a part of you. Whatever spirit is involved with them, will get involved with you.

If you feed on their teaching extensively and they are in doctrinal error, you can get taken up with the same spirit and the same error. If a person is in doctrinal error, he is being motivated by other spirits than the Holy Spirit.

Just follow God, Jesus, the Holy Ghost, and be rooted and grounded in the Word for yourself. You can read after others, of course. But don't get taken up with the same spirit they have if they are not walking scripturally in the light of God's Word.

These are examples of foretelling through the word of wisdom in the prophet's office to *privately* warn someone. Also, the word of wisdom occasionally operates through a prophet in *public* to prepare people for what is ahead.

However, keep in mind that the main emphasis of a New Testament prophet will be forthtelling — preaching or teaching the Word of God.

Chapter 10
God Does Not Put Novices
In Positions of Authority

People sometimes ask the question, "Why do we call pastors by their title, but not the other four ministry gifts?" When I first came over among Pentecostal circles in 1937, in our part of the country we'd very often call ministers by their title or office. For instance, we would say, "Prophet So-and-so."

We don't do that so much today, and in one way it gives the impression that these offices no longer function in the Body of Christ. Yet in our day if we did use ministry titles, without scriptural teaching along this line, some people would invariably get into a ditch and get into trouble. I never wanted to be called a prophet myself, because I didn't want to be classed with the false ones. Someone asked me what a false prophet is. For one thing, a false prophet is someone who is trying to operate in that office when he is not called to that office.

Even if a person is a true prophet, it's not always wise to use titles because as I said, usually people get carried away with that. Besides, the ministry doesn't consist in name and title. It consists in power and demonstration of the Holy Ghost. It shouldn't matter to us what people call us or don't call us. We should just want to obey God.

What *is* important is that people stand in the ministry office they are called to in the power of the Holy Ghost and that their ministry is based solidly on the Word of God. We need all the ministries God has placed in the Body of Christ, no matter what we *label* them.

Some who do use the title "prophet" today are little more than novices in the ministry. People need to understand that God is not going to put a novice in that office. He's going to prove the minister first before He puts him in any ministry office. And many folks never even move into the fullness of their real calling or ministry in God because they are too unfaithful in the little that God has given them to do.

Jesus said something to me once about this, and it has become more real to me all the time. He said, "Spiritual growth is similar to natural growth."

For example, you knew some things as a teenager and you carried some responsibility. But it was different when you grew up and began being fully responsible as an adult. The same thing is true spiritually.

Those whom God calls to the ministry don't usually get into these offices all at once. Believers don't normally start out in the ministry God eventually has for them. There may be some exceptions to that, but as a normal rule that is true.

We see some reference to this in the Scriptures in Paul's ministry. Paul didn't start out in the ultimate ministry God had for him, which was the apostolic ministry. He was a prophet and a teacher for many years before God separated him for the greater work of the apostolic ministry (Acts 13:1,2).

If you are called to the ministry, don't think you will be the exception to the rule. No, God will prove you before He puts you in the office He has for you.

For example, if God calls you to pastor a church, you may eventually pastor a church of four thousand, but you couldn't start out there. You may have to start out with a congregation of four or forty and build up to four hundred. Actually, you wouldn't be qualified to pastor a church of four thousand when you first start out in the ministry.

It's the same way with the evangelist. He may have to start preaching to just a few people like I did or in the jails. Teachers may have to start out teaching in home meetings. And it may be that they never develop beyond that stage because that is all God has called them to do — it is the ultimate call God has for them.

But the point is, each one called to the fivefold ministry must prove himself faithful right where he is before God can use him to a greater degree. God can't increase the anointing on a person if he is not faithful to what God has already told him to do.

People don't normally start out in the ministry God ultimately has for them because there is a training and a proving time in God. Since spiritual growth is similar to natural growth, a person needs to grow and mature both naturally and spiritually before God will put him in a ministry office because ministry offices carry great responsibility.

God doesn't put novices, those who are untrained and immature in spiritual things, in positions of authority (1 Tim. 3:6).

Phases of Ministry

For example, in my own life, God didn't immediately move me into the office of the prophet. In fact, I had been in the ministry more than fifteen years before I stood in the office of the prophet.

I felt the call to preach all my life, of course. And after I was born again on the bed of sickness, I said, "Lord, You get me up from here and I'll go preach." I knew I was called to the ministry. I left that bed preaching and for years I was just anointed to preach. From 1934 until June 1943 — nine years — I was strictly a preacher.

In the early days of my ministry, I didn't like to teach. However, as a pastor, I had to teach the adult Bible class. But I was never so glad when it was over so I could preach again. I thought I wasn't anointed unless I was waving my arms like a windmill and spitting cotton.

But in June 1943 at three o'clock in the afternoon, the Lord dropped the teaching gift down into my spirit. Ephesians 4:7 says, ". . . *unto every one of us is given grace according to the measure of the gift of Christ.*"

You remember, in the Old Testament God told Elijah the prophet to anoint Elisha to be prophet "in his room" or in his stead (1 Kings 19:16). Elijah passed by Elisha and threw his mantle on him.

The mantle was an outer cloak which symbolized the anointing of God coming upon a person to stand in a particular office or to perform a particular task or function for God.

As I was walking across the floor that afternoon, the

teaching mantle fell upon me. It felt just like someone dropped a cloak on me, first on the outside, and then it went down on the inside of me into my spirit. I knew exactly what had happened. God gave me the ability to teach. I said out loud, "Now I can teach."

But I didn't go around telling people about that experience, saying, "I've got a teaching gift. I'm a teacher."

Become what God has called you to be first, and then people will see the anointing of God upon you. The spiritual equipment operating in your life will demonstrate what you are called to do. And you won't have to advertise it either. It will be readily apparent to everyone the office you stand in.

So I was a preacher and then a teacher of the Word, and I pastored for nearly twelve years. But I still didn't stand in the office of the prophet. Occasionally the word of wisdom was manifested through me. I interpreted tongues, but I didn't prophesy.

The word of knowledge began operating in my life consistently when I was baptized in the Holy Spirit. But I didn't operate it; it operated as the Spirit willed. But that still didn't make me a prophet.

The word of knowledge was a great blessing to me as a pastor. Many times when I was pastoring, minutes before a church member would drive up to the parsonage, by the word of knowledge I would tell my wife who was about to come to the door, why he was coming, and what his need was. A few minutes later that very person drove up and began talking about the exact thing the Lord had showed me.

That didn't happen every day, but it occurred consistently — almost every week. And if any of my church members got into trouble, I knew it immediately by the Spirit of God. The word of knowledge ought to operate in every pastor's life. I believe it would if pastors knew how to be sensitive to the Holy Spirit and how to yield to Him. But that still wouldn't make them prophets.

What often happens is that the word of knowledge operates occasionally in someone's life, and then they try to operate it at will to make something happen. When they do that, they unconsciously begin to yield to wrong spirits, and they get into trouble spiritually.

But even though the word of knowledge operated in my life on a consistent basis, I didn't step into the office of the prophet until 1952.

Actually, in 1950 Jesus appeared to me, and He said this to me: "When you left your last church, at that time, you entered into the first phase of the ministry I had for you."

I replied, "You mean I'm just now entering into the first phase after being in the ministry fifteen years?"

Jesus said, "Yes."

Then He made this comment: "Some ministers live and die and never even enter into the first phase of the ministry I have for them. That's the reason many of them, not all of them, but many of them die young and don't live their full length of time out down here."

Jesus explained that if you are not in the will of

God, then to some extent, you are in disobedience. When you are in disobedience, Satan can attack you. He has a right to attack you when you are in disobedience because you are on his territory.

I've experienced the difference between being in God's perfect will and being just in His permissive will! His perfect will is so much better!

Of course there will be tests and trials as long as we are on this earth. But if you're in the perfect will of God, He will see you through every one of them.

If you're not in the perfect will of God, you open a door to the devil. And you will have to repent and obey God before He can move in your behalf as He desires. It's just better to be in the perfect will of God.

Anyway, in 1952 Jesus appeared to me in a vision, and said, "From this time forward what is known in My Word as discerning of spirits will operate in your life and ministry when you are in the Spirit."

When I received the gift of discerning of spirits, I could see and hear in the realm of the spirit *when I was in the Spirit*. Then two revelation gifts — discerning of spirits and the word of knowledge — operated in my life consistently, plus prophecy.

Did they operate every day or every week? Not necessarily. Every service? No, it was as the Holy Spirit willed (1 Cor. 12:11). But it was then that I stepped into the office of the prophet.

But, you see, the point I'm trying to make is that God doesn't put those whom He has called to the full-time ministry in these ministry offices overnight. When Jesus appeared to me in 1952 and the gift of discerning of spirits began to operate in my ministry and I entered into the prophetic office, I had been in the ministry more than fifteen years. Even then, I didn't stand in that office publicly until 1953.

But I still didn't advertise that I stood in the office of the prophet, and I don't mention it much today. A person who has to advertise his calling, doesn't have much.

It's all right to advertise your meetings, of course, and let folks know you're in town. But if you are called to the office of the prophet, you don't have to broadcast it all over town. People will find out soon enough if you are really called to that office by the supernatural equipment that operates through you.

Where novices get into trouble is that they go out and tell everyone they are called to a ministry office when they've never even operated in that office or they are just a beginner in it!

As the old saying goes, "The proof of the pudding is in the eating." Are you first and foremost a preacher or a teacher of the Word? Do your prophecies come to pass? Do they line up with the Word of God? Are you teachable and easy to be entreated? Or do you cause strife and problems everywhere you go and get run off from every church where you preach?

These are the true tests of your ministry. Let your ministry first be proved. The Bible says, ". . . *let every man prove his own work, and then shall he have rejoic-*

ing in himself alone . . ." (Gal. 6:4).

Just because gifts of the Spirit operate through you occasionally, that doesn't make you a prophet. Any Spirit-filled believer may have an occasional manifestation of revelation gifts as the need arises. After all, the Holy Ghost is in believers, and He manifests Himself through the gifts of the Spirit to meet the needs of people.

But there is a vast difference between an occasional manifestation of a revelation gift and a person who is called to a fivefold *ministry* office through whom spiritual gifts operate on a *more consistent* basis. That's where some folks are missing it today.

Of course, the Bible encourages all believers to covet to prophesy. First Corinthians 14:31 says, ". . . *ye may all prophesy one by one. . . .*" But there are no revelation gifts — word of knowledge, word of wisdom, discerning of spirits — manifested in the simple gift of prophecy.

For example, in Acts 21:9 it says that Philip had four daughters "which did prophesy." But they didn't stand in the office of the prophet just because they prophesied.

Some folks see a prophet operate in some of the more spectacular demonstrations of the revelation gifts of the Spirit, and they think they can do that too. Then they try to prophesy using revelation gifts, and they are either prophesying in the flesh or they are inspired by occult powers.

Folks who are called to the office of the prophet are called to a full-time ministry *office.* They are called and set apart by *God* to the ministry. They can't call themselves or set themselves in a ministry office.

No Prophets in the Laity

You see, that's why there are no prophets among what we call the laity. Those in the laity aren't spiritually equipped, nor do they have the anointing to stand in a ministry office.

Some people among the laity claim they are prophets, but they aren't. They can't be because that is a ministry *office*, equipped supernaturally by God with spiritual gifts or *endowments*. Only God can equip a person with spiritual gifts and set him into a ministry office.

Ministry offices are for those called to the full-time ministry. The prophet is a ministry gift to the Body of Christ. Of course, a person called to the ministry can stand in more than one office, as he is called by God and equipped by the Holy Spirit.

However, pastors are not normally called to the office of the prophet for several reasons. First, there is no record in the Bible of a pastor who was also a prophet.

Second, the prophet's ministry seems to be more of a roving ministry, like that of the evangelist's ministry. For example, in the Old Testament, the prophet Samuel taught in a circuit (1 Sam. 7:16) and traveled from place to place.

Third, when a pastor is called to the pastoral office, that is his first calling or ministry. You understand that as the need might arise, God could move a pastor over into the prophetic ministry temporarily at times to minister. But that would not be his main call. The pastoral ministry is his first priority.

Pastors may even operate sometimes in revelation gifts, but that doesn't make them prophets. And God may at times temporarily put one who will eventually stand in the prophetic office in the pastoral office as part of his training, as he did with me.

The office of the prophet is a distinct office, equipped with a more *consistent* manifestation of revelation gifts of the Spirit. And it would be a person's main ministry, just as pastoring is the pastor's main ministry.

Let God Set You in Your Place In the Body of Christ

If you think God has called you to a ministry office, even the office of the prophet, let *Him* put you into that office. You couldn't step into it immediately anyway. You wouldn't be ready for it, and you would make a mess of it if you tried to put yourself into that office. But God will add to your spiritual maturity here a little and there a little as He sees fit.

If God *does* want to set you into the office of the prophet, allow *Him* to do it. As you are faithful to do what He gives you as you are maturing spiritually, eventually when He sees He can trust you with it, He will set you into that office.

If you are a novice in spiritual things, just be faithful to do what God has called you to do *today*. Be diligent to *"Study to shew thyself approved unto God, a workman that needeth not to be ashamed, rightly dividing the word of truth"* (2 Tim. 2:15).

There was a reason the Spirit of God said through the Apostle Paul not to put a novice in an office. A novice is too easily lifted up in pride, and that opens a door to the devil: *". . . lest being lifted up with pride he fall into the condemnation of the devil"* (1 Tim. 3:6).

Many novices have tried to enter the office of the prophet themselves. Many were lifted up in pride when Satan tempted them, and their lives and ministries were destroyed. Some probably sensed the calling of God in their spirits to the prophet's office, but instead of waiting for God to set them in that office, they tried to rush into it themselves.

Also, the Body of Christ needs to realize that ministering in the office of the prophet carries an awesome responsibility; that is one reason it isn't for novices.

Some folks say, "I wish *I* could operate in the office of the prophet." Oh, dear Lord! If they really had the opportunity, they probably wouldn't wish that because of the awesome responsibility that goes along with it.

For example, it is an awesome responsibility to look out over a congregation, and by the gifts of the Spirit see someone whom you know is going to die that very night.

Sometimes you know why they are going to die, and sometimes you don't. It takes the wisdom of God and the leading of the Holy Spirit to know what to do with that knowledge. You don't always tell the person what you know, unless you are specifically instructed to by the Lord.

It is the hardest thing in the world to minister over in the prophetic office sometimes because of some of the things you see and know by the Spirit of God.

I've been in meetings where I've stood in the office of the prophet and looked out over the congregation and seen into the realm of the Spirit. Many times I've seen exactly what was physically wrong with people.

And sometimes as the Spirit of God wills, I know the reason they are sick. It is an awesome responsibility to be used in revelation gifts of the Spirit and minister accurately according to the Holy Spirit's leading. Folks, this office is not for novices!

That's why you need to let God develop *you* and *your ministry*, whatever it may be. As God prepares you, people will recognize the gift of God in you. If you think God has called you to the prophetic office, study and show yourself approved, grow and mature spiritually, and be faithful as you serve Him in other capacities. God will mature you and prove you before he puts you in positions of increased responsibility.

Just trust in the wisdom of God and know that as you do your part and prepare yourself in the Word, God in His wisdom will do His part. He will lead and guide you, and if you are called to that office, He will mature you both naturally and spiritually first before *He* sets you into that office.

SECTION III

PASTORS

Chapter 11
Church Government

. . . When he [Jesus] *ascended up on high, he led captivity captive, and GAVE GIFTS UNTO MEN. . . .*

And he GAVE some, apostles; and some, prophets; and some, evangelists; and some, PASTORS and teachers.

— Ephesians 4:8,11

And God HATH SET SOME IN THE CHURCH, first apostles, secondarily prophets, thirdly teachers, after that miracles, then gifts of healings, helps, GOVERNMENTS, diversities of tongues.

— 1 Corinthians 12:28

Some people today are confused about church government and what constitutes correct church government. Church government refers to who is in authority in the local church and who is responsible for the leadership of the local body. How is the local church supposed to be run?

When you study the New Testament, you won't find any ironclad laws about church government. The New Testament is not as clear as we'd like it to be on this subject. And no matter what kind of church government a church has, a person can take scriptures out of their setting to try to prove that his particular kind of church government is right. Many arguments and "religious wars" have been waged over this issue.

Although there may be some gray areas in the Bible as far as what constitutes proper church government, there are some basic principles and guidelines laid down for us in the New Testament. If we stay within those guidelines, we will be fine. But if we get out beyond those basic principles, we are going to get into trouble.

The reason some confusion exists in this area is that some people have tried to take the things which Paul said about *ministry*, and make them apply to church *government*. But we need to understand that many ministries exist which have nothing to do with the governing of the local church.

You see, Paul talks about the fivefold *ministries* that are given to the Church, or *set* in the Church. These are people whom God has called and set in the Church to minister to the Body of Christ.

In Ephesians 4:11 and First Corinthians 12:28, Paul lists the fivefold *ministries*. The list of ministry gifts in Ephesians 4:11 is obvious: *apostles*, *prophets*, *evangelists*, *pastors*, and *teachers*.

And in First Corinthians 12:28, the offices of the *apostle*, *prophet*, and *teacher* are listed clearly enough. But we don't readily see the offices of the evangelist and pastor. However, the office of the *evangelist* is referred to in this list as "miracles" and "gifts of healings," since those manifestations frequently accompany that office, although they are not exclusive to that office. And the *pastoral* office is found in the word "governments."

Paul does not specifically mention church government except in this passage in First Corinthians 12:28 when he uses the word "governments," referring to the pastoral office.

We know that the word "governments" refers to a *ministry gift* because in this passage Paul is listing the ministry gifts, and he does not change his subject. Therefore, "governments" is a distinct ministry gift, *not* a combination of all the ministry gifts together, forming some kind of a church government.

Some people have interpreted this word "governments" to mean that Paul is saying all the ministry gifts make up church government. They claim that *all* the ministry gifts are found in this office of governments; therefore, they mistakenly say that all the ministry gifts are to *rule* and *govern* the local church.

In other words, according to this erroneous teaching, in order to have correct church government, the fivefold ministry must operate in every local church, no matter how small. And because the apostle and prophet are listed first, that means they have preeminence over all the other ministry gifts, including the pastor.

Because they assume that Paul lists the ministry gifts in the order of their importance and prominence in regard to *church government*, the pastoral office must not be very important because it is found fourth in this list in Ephesians 4:11 and not at all in the passage in

First Corinthians 12:28.

Therefore, according to this reasoning, every local church must have an apostle and a prophet in authority over the pastor to govern, lead, and guide the pastor and the congregation. They say that the apostle *governs* the sheep, including the pastor; the prophet *guides* the sheep, including the pastor; and the pastor *shepherds* the sheep under the leadership of an apostle and prophet.

That is unscriptural. In the first place, they have taken Paul's statement out of context to come up with the idea that all the ministry gifts make up the government of a local church.

In the second place, Paul isn't listing ministry gifts in their order of importance. If he were listing them by their importance, it would mean that the apostle, prophet, and evangelist are more important than the pastor and have authority over him in the local body. That doesn't line up with other scriptures on this subject.

In the third place, as we've already discussed, apostles are not set in the Body of Christ to govern other ministry gifts.

And the prophet isn't to *guide* anyone either. You won't find anywhere in the New Testament, even in the Early Church, where prophets guided anyone. Besides, why would the prophet have to guide the pastor? A pastor doesn't need an intermediary or a go-between in order to hear from God. The pastor has the Holy Spirit, too, and he can get direction for the church and guidance directly from God for himself.

When the Lord set the pastoral gift in the church, that means God will speak primarily to the pastor — not to the apostle or prophet — regarding the direction of that local body.

I cannot agree with the idea that the apostle and prophet are to rule over the pastor, or that each local body needs to have the fivefold ministry in operation in order to have proper New Testament church government.

"Governments" is listed separately, indicating that it is a distinct office from the other ministry gifts. As its own separate *office*, "governments" indicates the pastoral office.

You see, people can make Scripture say anything they want if they don't rightly divide the Word. But one of the simplest rules of Bible interpretation is to determine *who* is doing the talking; *to whom* is he talking; and *what* is he talking about. *Paul* was talking *to* believers *about* ministry gifts.

People get off into doctrinal error when they take one scripture, or a part of a scripture, and try to build a doctrine on it.

The Development of the Local Church

The only way to get a scriptural perspective of the error that is being taught in the Church today about apostles and prophets governing the local church, is to study the development of the local church in the Book of Acts. What was the origin of the local church, and how did church government evolve?

You see, at first the only local church was the church at Jerusalem. We have no record of the Church in its earliest days even evangelizing outside of Jerusalem. The local body was confined to the Jerusalem church.

But before Jesus ascended, He had told the disciples they were to be witnesses of Him in Jerusalem, Judaea, Samaria, and to the uttermost parts of the earth (Acts 1:8). In other words, the gospel was to be preached and works were to be started in other areas as well. However, years later the Early Church still hadn't done that; they had just stayed right there in Jerusalem. So for a period of time, the Jerusalem church was the only church in existence.

Therefore, for some years preaching and teaching in the Early Church was done by the Apostles of the Lamb, and initially all ministry was confined to the Jerusalem church. But when persecution arose, the Early Church went out witnessing. Although the apostles stayed in Jerusalem when the Church was scattered, later the apostles began establishing works in other areas.

The first record we have that believers left Jerusalem to evangelize is in Acts 8:1, and that occurred some years after Pentecost.

ACTS 8:1
1 ... And at that time there was a great persecution against the church which was at Jerusalem; and they were all SCATTERED ABROAD through-

out the REGIONS OF JUDAEA and SAMARIA,
except the apostles.

It was only after the persecution that believers went
out witnessing, and works began to be established in
other areas. It says the Church was "scattered abroad"
preaching the gospel. The Early Church finally obeyed
what Jesus had told them to do in Acts 1:8 by spreading
the good news about Him to others.

As new works were started outside of Jerusalem,
when doctrinal disputes arose, the disciples would
return to the Jerusalem church to settle these issues.

Development of Church Doctrine
In the Early Church

For example, in Acts 15, the apostles returned to
the Jerusalem church to settle matters of doctrine.

ACTS 15:1,2,4-6
1   And certain men which came down from
Judaea taught the brethren, and said, EXCEPT YE
BE CIRCUMCISED AFTER THE MANNER OF
MOSES, YE CANNOT BE SAVED.
2   When therefore Paul and Barnabas had no
small dissension and disputation with them, they
determined that Paul and Barnabas, and certain
other of them, should go up to JERUSALEM [the
mother church] unto the APOSTLES and ELDERS
about this question....
4   And when they were come to Jerusalem, they
were received of the church, and of the APOS-
TLES and ELDERS, and they declared all things
that God had done with them.

> 5   But there rose up certain of the sect of the
> Pharisees which believed, saying, That it was
> needful to circumcise them, and to command them
> to keep the law of Moses.
> 6   And the APOSTLES and ELDERS came together
> for to consider of this matter.

Some people use Acts 15 to try to prove that all the
ministry gifts governed the local body. But this passage
doesn't have anything to do with local church government. In other words, it had nothing to do with the
daily running of the church and who was in authority
in the local body.

Acts 15 is an account of the New Testament Church
in its early stages of development. In these early stages
of development, all the ministry gifts worked together
to decide universal church doctrine.

For example, regarding matters of circumcision,
those in ministry offices decided whether believers
needed to be circumcised according to the Law of Moses
to be saved. Although all the ministry gifts helped
decide this issue, all the ministry gifts did not *govern*
the local church.

"Elders" here signifies pastors and those called to
the fivefold ministry. You see, when a minister is
ordained, he is ordained to full eldership in the Body of
Christ. Every ordained minister is an elder.

Notice that a deacon board or a group of businessmen
elected to a church board did not decide spiritual issues.

ACTS 15:22-30
22 Then pleased it the APOSTLES and ELDERS,
with the WHOLE CHURCH, to send chosen men of

their own company to Antioch with Paul and
Barnabas; namely, Judas surnamed Barsabas, and
Silas, chief men among the brethren:
23 And they wrote letters by them after this manner; The APOSTLES and ELDERS and BRETH-
REN send greeting unto the brethren which are of
the Gentiles in Antioch and Syria and Cilicia.
24 Forasmuch as we have heard, that certain
which went out from us have troubled you with
words, subverting your souls, saying, Ye must be
circumcised, and keep the law: to whom we gave
no such commandment:
25 It seemed good unto us, being assembled with
ONE ACCORD, to send chosen men unto you with
our beloved Barnabas and Paul,
26 Men that have hazarded their lives for the
name of our Lord Jesus Christ.
27 We have sent therefore Judas and Silas, who
shall also tell you the same things by mouth.
28 For it seemed good to the Holy Ghost, and to
us, to lay upon you no greater burden than these
necessary things;
29 That ye abstain from meats offered to idols,
and from blood, and from things strangled, and
from fornication: from which if ye keep yourselves, ye shall do well. Fare ye well.
30 So when they were dismissed, they came to
Antioch: and when they had gathered the multitude together, they delivered the epistle.

Even though those in the fivefold ministries helped
decide doctrinal issues in the early development of the
Church, it doesn't say, "The fivefold ministry *governed*
the church." It just says the fivefold ministry was set *in*
the Church (1 Cor. 12:28). They all had specific functions, but not all offices had the function of "govern-

ments." That was a distinct office with its own function.

Actually, the apostles, elders, and the entire Church at Jerusalem had something to say in deciding some matters (Acts 15:22,23). For instance, the whole church was in agreement with the apostles' and elders' decision regarding church doctrine, and they all decided who to send with Paul and Barnabas.

Of course, as the pastor or overseer of the Jerusalem church, James presided over the meeting (Acts 15:13). And even though the other ministry gifts had their input, notice that as the pastor, James ultimately made the final decision (Acts 15:13,19-21).

The Development of Elders in the Early Church

At first the Early Church didn't have pastors; the only recognized ministry they had was found in those men the Bible refers to as the Apostles of the Lamb. When the apostles went out from the Jerusalem church, they ministered primarily to the Jews.

Then in the course of time, God raised up Paul to go to the Gentiles. We can learn much about the development of the local church in other areas outside of Jerusalem by looking at Paul's ministry. On his missionary journeys when Paul was establishing churches, the longest period of time he stayed in one place preaching the gospel was three years (Acts 20:31), but normally he stayed a shorter time than that (Acts 18:11).

It seems that Paul would stay long enough in an

area to get the people established in faith and to start a church. But every church he left was still a baby church in the infancy stages of development. It takes time for ministries to be established and for churches to grow and develop spiritually.

So when Paul or one of the apostles started a new work, they would choose one or more of the older men in the congregation to oversee the work. The Greek word "elder" literally means *an older person.*

But if these men weren't called to the fivefold ministry, they wouldn't have any anointing on them to stand in a ministry office. And if they weren't developed in spiritual things, they would still be novices. It takes time to grow and develop spiritually. But mature men with some natural wisdom *could* oversee the new work until God had the time to raise up qualified men to stand in the pastoral office.

So in the process of time, many of these elders or older men who were actually called to the ministry developed and matured spiritually and became qualified and spiritually equipped to stand fully in the pastoral office.

Therefore, in the process of time, as the Early Church grew and developed spiritually, it was possible to have men who were called of God and spiritually equipped as pastors to take the oversight of the flock. It was no longer necessary to select someone simply on the basis of age or maturity; there was a recognition of those who were actually called to and equipped for the ministry.

Sometimes people say, "Let's just go back and do

things the way they did in the Early Church." But if we do that, we will have a baby Church — a Church still in its infancy stages of development. It would be unscriptural for the Church today at this stage of development to randomly take people from the congregation and give them oversight of the church, unless of course it was just a temporary situation until one who was actually called and anointed as a pastor could be set in office.

Of course, in *doctrine* we are the same as the Early Church. We have the same new birth, the same baptism of the Holy Spirit, and the same Lord's Supper. But we won't necessarily be the same in *practice* in the sense that we won't do things the same way they did as far as the growth and development of the Church is concerned. You see, the Early Church was in its first stages of development, and we aren't. The fivefold ministry is already developed in the Church today.

Let's look at the church at Ephesus to see how that local church developed. The church at Ephesus had its beginning when Paul came to Ephesus many years after the Day of Pentecost and preached the gospel to the disciples there (Acts 19:1-7).

Those Ephesians were just disciples; they had been baptized by John the Baptist, who told them to believe on Jesus Christ who was to come. But the Ephesian disciples didn't know that Jesus had already come, so they weren't born again.

When Paul told them Jesus had come, they believed on Jesus and were born again. Then Paul laid his hands on them, and they were filled with the Holy

Spirit (Acts 19:6,7). That was the beginning of the church at Ephesus.

Then years later, Paul called together the elders of the church at Ephesus and gave them instruction about feeding the flock of God.

> **ACTS 20:17,28**
> **17 And from Miletus he sent to Ephesus, and called the ELDERS of the church. . . .**
> **28 Take heed therefore unto yourselves, and to all the flock, over the which the Holy Ghost hath made you OVERSEERS, to FEED THE CHURCH OF GOD, which he hath purchased with his own blood.**

Here Paul addressed them as "elders" and "overseers." You see, by this time the church had had time to grow and develop, and the elders were no longer just older men. They were true elders in the spiritual sense of the term. They were overseers, or pastors.

By this time, the Holy Ghost had developed teachers and preachers of the Word and "set" them in the Church. That's why Paul instructed these elders to ". . . *feed the church of God. . . .*" These "elders" were now true pastors who had the pastoral oversight of the local body and the ability to feed the people spiritually.

Paul couldn't be just talking to older men here, because an older man with no anointing on him for the ministry wouldn't be spiritually equipped to feed God's people the Word of God.

In the early days of my ministry, I saw an example of an older man being put in charge of a church until

God raised up a man called to the pastoral ministry. This occurred in one of the churches I later pastored.

Before I pastored that particular church, a layman named Brother Flagler had been installed as an elder in the church. He was an older Christian, one of the first ones to be saved in that congregation. He had the oversight of running the church until the Lord raised up a pastor for that congregation.

Brother Flagler readily admitted, "I can't preach. I'm not called to preach or to pastor. I did teach a Sunday school class in the church. But I just sort of took charge of the church until God brought us a pastor. Sometimes we would go for almost a year without a pastor, but we just kept having church. I would bring a minister in to preach in the services, and I would oversee the running of the church. But I had no anointing to teach or preach, and I wasn't called to pastor."

In the course of time, God raised up a pastor for that church. But in the meantime Brother Flagler acted as an overseer of the work.

That's exactly what happened in the Early Church. An older man or an older believer was put in charge of the church until God had time to develop the ministry gifts of the pastor who would then become an elder or overseer in the true sense — a shepherd of God's sheep.

'Governments'

Studying the development of the Early Church helps us see that the word "governments" in First

Corinthians 12:28 is referring to the pastoral office. Ask yourself the question, *Who governs the local body*? The pastor does. Nowhere in Scripture do we find the government of a local body headed up by the apostle, prophet, evangelist, or teacher.

And "governments" or *the governing of the local church* is certainly not found in the sheepfold, among the sheep. It couldn't be, because "governments" is referring to a ministry gift office, and laymen are not spiritually equipped to stand in ministry offices. Laymen have no anointing upon them to minister in the fivefold offices. No, the shepherd governs the local body.

We also know the office of "governments' is *not* found in the office of the apostle because nowhere in the New Testament do we find apostles governing the local body. In fact, the office of the apostle couldn't be part of the church government because the apostolic office is typically not a stationary ministry located just in the local body.

An apostle should be a member of a local body, of course, but he doesn't stay right there in the local church, because one of the outstanding characteristics of an apostle is that he is a sent one. He is sent out with a message, or to pioneer new works and new churches, or to minister in the mission field.

No, the *shepherd* governs the sheep in the local body! You can go over to Israel today and see the shepherd with his sheep. He takes care of the sheep and watches over them; he *governs* them. If you told him, "I have authority over this flock, and I am going to sell all your sheep," that shepherd would send you on your way!

No one else has authority over a shepherd's flock. The shepherd has the authority and responsibility to *govern* the flock because he is entrusted by God with the oversight of the flock.

It is the same way in the local body. The governing of the flock is done by the shepherd of that local congregation because he is the overseer of the local church. We are not talking about a natural, human governing or government. We are talking about a divine spiritual oversight, which provides for the nurturing of the sheep in an attitude of love.

ACTS 20:28
28 Take heed therefore unto yourselves, and to all the flock, over the which the Holy Ghost hath made you OVERSEERS, to feed the church of God, which he hath purchased with his own blood.

The words "shepherd" and "pastor" come from the same Greek word, "poimen." *Vine's Expository Dictionary of New Testament Words* gives us the definition of the word "poimen" or shepherd:

A shepherd, one who tends herds or flocks (not merely one who feeds them), is used metaphorically of Christian "pastors." Pastors guide as well as feed the flock.[1]

The same Greek word that is translated "overseer" in Acts 20:28 is translated "bishop" in First Timothy 3:1. It is the Greek word "episkopos," and it is translated *superintendent, bishop,* or *overseer*, and according to *Vine's* is another term for "elder."

So it's safe to say that the *bishop, overseer, shepherd, pastor,* and *elder* all describe the pastoral office. There are some places in the New Testament where the term "elder" may also apply to other offices as well, but the Bible is talking to pastors, overseers, or shepherds in Acts 20:28 when it says, *"Take heed unto yourselves, and to all the flock. . . ."* The word "flock" refers to sheep. Sheep must have a shepherd.

It is true that the word "pastor" is only used one time in the New Testament, and that is in this passage in Ephesians 4:11: *"And he gave some, apostles . . . prophets . . . evangelists . . . PASTORS and teachers."*

However, the word "pastor" in its varying forms — *bishop, elder, overseer,* and *shepherd* — is used many times throughout the New Testament.

The Bible has much to say about sheep and shepherds. Jesus used the word "shepherd" Himself many times. For instance, Jesus said, *"I am the good shepherd . . ."* (John 10:11,14). Jesus is the Chief Shepherd (1 Peter 5:4), and the pastor is the undershepherd of God's flock; he shepherds and feeds the flock of God under the direction of the Chief Shepherd, the Lord Jesus Christ, the Head of the Church.

Actually, the original Greek of Ephesians 4:11, "pastors and teachers," seems to indicate that the offices of pastor and teacher can function together. In other words, a pastor can also be a teacher. And there are those who are called specifically to be pastor-teachers.

Reading through the New Testament, I can't find any higher office in the local church than the pastoral office. I've read the New Testament through more than 150 times, and I've never seen a higher authority in the local church than the pastoral office.

You will find in studying church history that every church that tried to build on the false foundation of apostles and prophets governing a church has come to nought. Because that is not scriptural, God can't bless it.

'Every *Wind* of Doctrine'

These erroneous teachings have torn up churches and hurt good people. Any genuine minister of the gospel, no matter what office he stands in, doesn't minister in such a way as to cause strife and to divide a church over doctrinal issues. If he doesn't come to a church to bless the people, then he's false; he is not a true minister of the gospel.

God doesn't want us to be children anymore. He wants us to grow up spiritually and to learn not to accept every wind of doctrine that someone is teaching in the Body of Christ.

> **EPHESIANS 4:14**
> **14 That we henceforth BE NO MORE CHILDREN, tossed to and fro, and carried about with every WIND OF DOCTRINE, by the sleight of men, and cunning craftiness, whereby they lie in wait to deceive.**

I want you to notice something in this passage of Scripture. The Bible says children are tossed about and deceived with "every *wind* of doctrine." It doesn't say children are tossed about or deceived with "every *wrong* doctrine."

Conybeare's translation says, ". . . blown round by every shifting current of teaching."

The *Amplified* translation says, ". . . wavering with every changing wind of doctrine, [the prey of] the cunning and cleverness of unscrupulous men . . . in every shifting form of trickery in inventing errors to mislead."

In other words, some people take biblical doctrine and pervert it slightly, and it deceives others. They put a wrong interpretation on what the Bible says, and spiritual children can get carried away with the error.

You can pervert doctrine by taking a portion of Scripture out of its context or setting by putting it with another scripture. The Bible calls that "the sleight of men" (Eph. 4:14). Error occurs when people manipulate, "wrest," or *twist* scriptures to make them say what they want them to say (2 Peter 3:16).

As I said, it's important to differentiate when the Bible is talking about the *Church at large* — the Body of Christ in general — and when it is talking about the *local church.*

All the ministry gifts function in the Church at large, in the Body of Christ as a whole. But you won't have all the ministry gifts functioning in each local church in order to constitute "correct" church government.

For example, at RHEMA Bible Church there is the senior pastor, Kenneth Hagin Jr., and five others on the pastoral staff, including two associate pastors, the youth and children's ministers and the minister of music. There are also thirty or more full-time traveling ministers — teachers and evangelists — who are members of the church. But they don't minister *in* the church; they all go out *from* the church, preaching and teaching the Word. They are not part of the church government.

The governing of RHEMA Bible Church is headed up in the pastoral staff. They are the ones who have the daily oversight and care of the church.

The traveling ministers are all in that one local body because they are members of RHEMA Bible Church, but they have nothing to do with the everyday running of the church. They don't even preach in the church unless called upon to do so. They are *in* the church, but their ministries require them to go out *from* the church to minister.

Also, we need to realize that some people's ministries require them to go out *from* the local body to the Church in general, whereas others are called to minister *in* their own local church body. Ministers need to know if the call of God on their lives is to stay in their own local church and minister, or if God is calling them to a traveling ministry to the Body of Christ at large.

Some teachers have missed it by thinking that because they are called to teach, that automatically means God wants them to minister throughout the Body of Christ at large. But God calls some teachers just to minister as a Sunday school teacher or a Bible teacher in some other capacity in their own local church. I have seen some marvelous anointings on teachers called to minister in the local church.

For example, one man in our home church in Texas was a marvelous Bible teacher. He taught a Bible class and had a great teaching anointing. Because he was so anointed, people used to say to him, "You ought to get out of this local body and travel to other churches and teach throughout the Body of Christ." He would always say, "No. That's not my call. My call is to teach right here in this local church."

There are other teachers who are called to a traveling type of ministry to the Body of Christ at large. They go from place to place, teaching the Word. That's their call in the Body of Christ. But it is up to each member in the Body of Christ to find out what his call is and to find out where God wants him to minister, and then be faithful to minister as God has instructed him.

----

[1] W. E. Vine, M.A., *An Expository Dictionary of New Testament Words* (Old Tappan, New Jersey: Fleming H. Revell Company, 1940), p. 167.

Chapter 12
The Pastor and
The Local Church

There are two primary organizations or institutions that God has put His approval on. Number one, the home and family. He instituted that first. Number two, the church. And really, the local church is like a family; it is a church family. Have you ever noticed that the family and the church are the two things the devil attacks more than anything else?

People are always asking, "What is God doing today?" as if God is going to do something new every day. One of the main things God is doing today is emphasizing the local church. But that's not new.

God has always put his blessing, approval, and emphasis on the local church, but because some of these things have gotten out of balance, He is *re*emphasizing the local church to let us know it is a priority with Him. Actually, God is just directing us back to where we ought to be.

I'll tell you exactly what God wants to do in the Body of Christ today. Number one, He wants to build strong local churches. Number two, he wants members of local churches to learn to flow in the Spirit.

We need to realize that Jesus Christ, the Head of the Church, is the One who instituted the local church and *set* the pastoral office in the Body of Christ. Notice something Jesus said about the pastoral office in

Matthew chapter 9.

> **MATTHEW 9:35,36**
> **35 And Jesus went about all the cities and vil-
> lages, teaching in their synagogues, and preaching
> the gospel of the kingdom, and healing every sick-
> ness and every disease among the people.**
> **36 But when he saw the multitudes, he was moved
> with compassion on them, because they fainted,
> and were scattered abroad, AS SHEEP HAVING
> NO SHEPHERD.**

In this passage, the Bible doesn't say that when Jesus saw the multitudes, He was moved with compassion because the people fainted as sheep without an *apostle* or *prophet*. It doesn't say the multitude fainted as sheep without an *evangelist* or *teacher*. No! It says that they fainted and were scattered abroad as sheep without a *shepherd*! Sheep need a shepherd.

Jesus knew the sheep would be scattered without a pastor. The evangelist and the teacher don't have the same anointing on them to take care of the sheep and nurture them.

No Substitute for the Local Church

That's the reason I take umbrage with some of these teachers who downgrade the local church and encourage folks to be independent from a church body. They leave the impression that folks don't need the local church.

One Bible teacher I knew actually said to several pastors, "I don't much believe in the local church. If folks will listen to me on radio and television and read

my books and listen to my tapes, they can stay home
and grow spiritually just as much as anyone who goes
to church."

That's not scriptural. By saying that, he did away
with the pastoral office, which *Jesus Christ*, the Head of
the Church, set in the local body! Folks may grow some
just by listening to tapes and television ministries, but it
will be a lopsided spiritual growth. They need a pastor — a shepherd. The shepherd holds a unique place in
the fivefold ministry because he is the one who has been
set in the Church by Jesus to nurture and tend the
sheep.

I said, "Isn't it awful that poor ole Jesus didn't know
that folks could grow spiritually with just the ministry
of teachers, so He went ahead and put shepherds in the
local body. Poor ole Jesus is not as smart as that fellow!
He must not have known what He was doing by setting
pastors in the Church."

But then this teacher admitted, "I don't like to be
around people and take care of their problems." But,
you see, that is a shepherd's job. A pastor is on call
twenty-four hours a day for the needs of the sheep.

When I say God put his approval on the *church*,
that means the local body, not someone's television ministry. That's not the church. That is just an arm of ministry, and it can never substitute for the local body. A
radio ministry can never take the place of the local
church, nor can crusades or seminars.

Radio and television ministries and crusades and
seminars are just supplements or outreaches of the
church; they are not the local church. People who think

they can quit going to church and just listen to television ministries and go to crusades and seminars is like someone trying to stay alive eating only vitamin supplements instead of food!

You can see how unreasonable it would be for someone to say, "I'm going to quit eating food and just take vitamins." No, if a person did that he would die.

It's the same way with the local church. If you quit going to church and just try to grow spiritually by relying on radio or television ministries for your spiritual diet, your spiritual health will suffer.

Some of these radio and television ministries want you to send them your tithes and offerings. I won't even listen to television or radio ministers who try to get people to send tithes to them. Actually, television and radio preachers shouldn't drain money away from the local church.

I'm not against Christians supporting other preachers if they think they are worthy. But television or radio ministries can't take the place of the local church and they shouldn't encourage folks to send their tithes to them.

I've told people for years, "Send your tithes to your local church. After you've paid your tithes and offerings to your local church, then you can send an offering to another ministry if you want to." I've never asked anyone to send me their tithes because I believe the tenth belongs to the local church (Lev. 27:32; Mal. 3:10).

When you are sick or in the hospital, do these television ministers who want your tithes and offerings come and minister to you? When you get married, do they come and counsel you and perform the ceremony? Do they help you in times of trouble and family bereavement? No!

No, the pastor is the one who performs those functions in the local church. And he is the one who makes sure the flock of God is fed a balanced spiritual diet. For that reason he holds a unique place among the sheep. He is like the daddy of a family. He loves the sheep in a way that an evangelist, prophet, or teacher can't love them because he has the shepherd's anointing on him.

You see, the evangelist can preach, but when the service is over, he can walk out the door. And the teacher and the prophet can come along and hold a teaching crusade at a church and teach the people, but when it's over, they can leave.

But the pastor can't leave the sheep that have been committed to his care, nor does he want to — not if he's a true shepherd. His ministry is stationary in the local body. He's got to stay right there with the people and help nurture them.

Let me say something else while I'm at it. Teaching centers cannot take the place of the local church. Some of these teaching centers have one or two services a week, but there is no shepherd, only a teacher. That's not having church.

A pastor will either be a preacher or a teacher of the Word, but his main office is to pastor. But if a minister just has the teaching gift, then his ministry gift is *teaching*, not the pastoral office. Just because a person can preach or teach, doesn't make him a shepherd.

A pastor can be a teacher, don't misunderstand me. But if a minister is just a teacher, and he isn't called to the pastoral office, then his teaching center can't take the place of the local church. If he's just a teacher, he ought to teach the people about getting into a good home church.

Then there are those fellows who claim to be pastors, but they run in and preach on Sunday morning and they're gone all the rest of the time. That's not a true shepherd! They ought to stay home and *pastor* their flock.

It's all right for a pastor to be gone once in a while. But for the most part a pastor ought to be in the local body tending the sheep. Some pastors wonder why their people aren't growing spiritually. Sometimes it's because the pastor isn't tending the sheep properly.

What has happened in the Body of Christ is that we have gotten some of these things out of balance. One reason we have gotten them out of balance is that many folks who came into the Charismatic Movement and got saved and filled with the Holy Ghost had not been raised in church. Some of them came out of the denominational church, but many really didn't know the purpose of the local church so they didn't esteem it properly.

As wonderful as crusades and seminars are for our spiritual growth and edification, they cannot take the place of the local church. You cannot run a church like you would a crusade or a seminar.

For example, when I'm holding a crusade, I usually leave the auditorium as soon as the service is over. The anointing is so strong, it is sometimes hard for the

physical body to stand up under it. I don't want to call
attention to myself, so I leave the services. As a traveling minister, I can leave the service immediately in a
crusade or a seminar.

But a pastor can't do that in the local assembly —
not if he is a true shepherd. When I was a pastor, I was
the first one in the church to greet the people, and I
was the last one to leave, shaking hands and fellow-
shipping with people after the service was over.

As a pastor, the people needed to know I was available and that I was there to serve them. You can't run a
church service like you do a seminar. You might have a
crusade *in* the church, and the minister holding the
crusade might act that way, but the pastor can't.
Besides, a pastor would rather minister to the needs of
the sheep than do anything else.

That's the reason it is readily apparent that some
folks aren't called to the pastoral office. They don't want
to be with the sheep.

I recently heard about a fellow who was supposedly
a pastor. But after several years, he was still only running twenty-five people in his congregation. It's no wonder because when he finished preaching, he would turn
and walk out the back door! That man either wasn't
called to the pastoral office, or he was misled as to the
true nature of the shepherd's role in the local body.
That's not the pastoral office in demonstration.

No, the true shepherd loves the sheep. He'd rather
die than to see them hurt. He wants to see the sheep
blessed and helped more than anything else.

The Local Church Is a Church Family

As a church family, the local church is going to have some of the same problems that any natural family will have because it's made up of people. The pastor will have to deal with those problems, whether it is discipline problems, financial problems, or any other kind of problems. It is not the job of some so-called apostle or prophet who doesn't even know the sheep to come in and start disciplining another man's sheep.

In the natural realm, children in a family sometimes get into disobedience and need a father's guidance. Sometimes the father of a family needs to provide correction. When your children need discipline, you don't call an outsider in to take care of disciplining them, do you? Of course not.

It's the same way in the local body. That local pastor is like the daddy of the local church. The sheep in a church body need the shepherd to nurture them with the Word of God and care for them in the sheepfold. And if they need discipline, they need a pastor who has their best interests at heart to administer biblical correction in a loving way.

The shepherd is the one who is qualified to correct the sheep spiritually if they need it because he is there all the time with them. He knows his congregation and has a genuine care and concern for their welfare. If his flock sometimes needs to be corrected, it is certainly *not* the teacher's responsibility, any more than it is the apostle's or prophet's responsibility, to come in and spiritually correct a pastor's church members.

No, people need a shepherd! They can't be perfected without the pastor of the local body. Actually, all the other ministry gifts would labor in vain if it weren't for the pastor, because he is the one who is responsible to tend, care for, and nurture the sheep with the Word of God. Sheep will never grow spiritually and never reach full maturity without a shepherd and the local church.

Because the local church is a family, the church ought to see after their own members, just as a family takes care of its own family members. If church members are sick and in the hospital, the pastoral staff ought to be right there to minister to them. When folks want to get married, the pastor is there to counsel them and perform the ceremony. When someone dies in a person's family, the pastor and that church family is right there to surround that family with love and support.

If you don't belong to a local church, or you only go once in a while, how would anyone in the church know if you needed prayer or were sick?

The benefit of the local church goes beyond just the spiritual side of life. The local church was also instituted by God to be a blessing to people on the natural side of life.

You see, there's the spiritual side of life, but there's also the natural side of life. You can't *just* live in the Spirit all the time; you're not supposed to because you're still living in the natural realm.

You've got to walk in the Spirit as you live in this natural world. Of course, the local church is to feed people spiritually, but it can also be a blessing to its members in certain natural ways too.

That's why the local church is so important. At one time or another in our lives, all of us need help in the natural realm as well as in the spiritual realm.

God puts each of us with a group of believers in the local body with whom we can fellowship and grow spiritually. And in times of trouble we all need those to whom we can turn for edification and comfort.

For example, who did the disciples go to in times of trouble? When they were thrown into jail, threatened, and finally released, the Bible says the disciples ". . . *went to their own COMPANY . . .*" (Acts 4:23).

Yes, you can turn in prayer requests to some other ministry, but sometimes you need more than prayer. Sometimes you need the fellowship of other believers of like faith; you need the physical presence of brothers and sisters around you, surrounding you with their faith and love.

A Pastor Is a *Shepherd* — Not a *Dictator*

The pastor of the local body is like the daddy of the local church. He's not to be a dictator. But sometimes it takes a man who is seasoned in patience to be the shepherd of the local body.

By pastoring God's sheep, a pastor learns some things about dealing with people he just can't learn any other way. Among other things, he learns some patience, and if he's wise, he will learn to love people just as they are.

I was talking to a certain minister who ten years before I got there had pastored the same church I was then pastoring. When he was the pastor, he had known one of my board members. At the time, this man was an unstable Christian.

The pastor told me, "When I pastored that church, that man had been saved and filled with the Holy Spirit for many years, yet he was the most unfaithful church member you ever saw. He rarely came to church, and he never put one dime in the offering. How in the world he ever turned out to be such a stalwart Christian, I don't know."

Then he added, "I'll tell you one thing. When he did show up for church, I was laying in wait for him!" That pastor gave himself away.

I replied, "That's the trouble. Even an old hog would have enough sense to quit coming to the feeding trough if you took a baseball bat and beat him in the head every time he came to eat! After you left, some of us pastors who came after you started feeding him spiritually with the Word, and he outgrew some of those babyhood traits of Christianity and developed into a stalwart Christian."

A pastor is always going to have baby Christians in his congregation. But he can't beat the sheep over the head to try to make them grow and develop! When I pastored, I was careful not to beat the sheep spiritually. I tried to see them through the eyes of faith as they could be, because I practiced walking by faith, not by sight.

Pastors need to learn to see their flock through the eyes of faith. If pastors walk by sight, many times from the pulpit they would probably want to skin people's hide, salt them down, and hang them on the wall to dry! But even in this area of spiritual growth, a pastor needs to walk by faith, not by sight. A good shepherd sees the people in his congregation as they could be with the right nurturing and spiritual diet.

How are the sheep going to mature and outgrow the babyhood stage of Christianity? By the pastor feeding them the right diet and treating them with love. That's how you see people through the eyes of faith. Then given time, they can become stalwart Christians. I know what I'm talking about because I practiced that as a pastor.

The shepherd has to give his life for the sheep, even in this area of seeing people through the eyes of faith, because that's not always easy.

A pastor has a grave responsibility to tend and nurture the sheep in a loving attitude. But having the oversight of the sheep doesn't mean lording it over people or mistreating them.

I remember a revival I held for a pastor once down in Texas. He was one of those hard-hitters who had the attitude, *Everyone is wrong but me.* He was legalistic and wouldn't allow a woman to sing in the choir if she had short hair or wore makeup.

But when I went back several years later to hold another revival at his church, his attitude had totally changed. I asked him what had happened to him.

He said, "I started seeking the Lord because over a seventeen-year period, none of the churches I'd pastored ever grew. The people supported me, and I'd always had plenty of money, even in Depression Days. I wasn't lacking, but none of the churches ever grew —

not in numbers or spiritually."

He said, "I began to fast and pray about it. I went over to the church guest quarters, and I told my wife, 'Don't disturb me because I'm going to fast and pray and seek God.' I stayed there five days fasting, just drinking water and seeking God in the Word and in prayer.

"I asked the Lord, 'Lord, what is wrong? I've been pastoring all these years, and not one of my churches has ever grown. We never get any new members and spiritually the people don't seem to grow.'"

The Lord answered me. He said, "One problem is that you kill off all the lambs, so you never have any full-grown sheep. Your congregation can't grow if you're continually killing all the lambs."

Jesus said, "You leave the lambs alone. Feed and nurture them, but just leave them to Me. They're going to romp around and run in and out, and sometimes they may run off yonder over the hill because they're little lambs. And you might even think they are gone for good. But before you know it, they'll come back. Just leave them alone."

"Not only that," Jesus said, "but you kill off all the sick sheep in your flock instead of nurturing them and taking care of them. If some of the people in your congregation need a spiritual operation, instead of praying for them and nurturing them, you butcher them up.

"In the natural, if one of your church members had something wrong with him, you might be able to find the problem by taking a butcher knife and opening him up and cutting out the infected area. But what kind of mess would he be in when you got through with him?

But spiritually speaking that's exactly what you do to your sick sheep!"

The Lord said, "You need to nurture sick sheep, not butcher them! You could get most of them healed if you'd give them the Word. And if any of them do need an 'operation,' you just leave that to Me, and let Me operate on them."

The Lord continued, "And, of course, you've done well financially because you kicked all the people out of the church who didn't pay tithes. So, of course, everyone in the church pays tithes."

This pastor said to the Lord, "Lord, I've been wrong. I repent. God, please forgive me."

Then this pastor said to me, "I repented to the Lord, and I changed. Since I've changed, the church has been growing."

Thank God for those with a true shepherd's heart. A good shepherd gives his life for the sheep (John 10:11). He puts them first. He is the one who has oversight of the sheep. He is the one in charge of the sheep and has the best interests of the sheep at heart.

In all the years I pastored, I always told the people, "If you find another church where you are fed better than you are here and can grow spiritually more than you can here, I encourage you to go there. In fact, I insist that you go because I've got your best interests at heart."

If pastors try to control people's lives and make them do what they want them to do, they will probably end up losing half of their congregation!

Soon after the Depression, I went to visit a certain

church. In those days, it was the first brick church I had ever heard of that was built by Pentecostal people. Most Pentecostals had a wooden-frame church. So I went by to visit that pastor.

I was about twenty-three years old, and the pastor was fifty-five years old. As I fellowshipped with him, he told me about another minister who had come into the area and was holding tent meetings. This pastor didn't agree with everything that minister taught.

This pastor said to me, "I'm going to get up in the Sunday service and forbid my people to go to that tent meeting." The minister who was holding the tent meeting basically taught sound doctrine, but there were some things he taught that didn't line up with the Word.

Even though I was a lot younger than this pastor, I knew he would be making a mistake by forbidding his congregation to go to these other meetings. But you don't tell folks everything you know, especially when you know they won't listen to you.

So the pastor got up in his Sunday morning service to forbid his people to go to that tent meeting. This situation was just an indication of his harsh, dictatorial attitude towards his sheep. In less than a year, that pastor not only lost his church, but he was out of the ministry. He never did get back into the ministry.

About a year after that happened, I was pastoring a church in that same vicinity. This same minister who had held the tent meetings began to hold tent meetings near my church. One of the other pastors in town came to me, and asked, "What are you going to do about that minister preaching in this area?"

I said, "Not one single thing. I'm not even going to mention it to my congregation."

The pastor said to me, "I'm going to forbid my people to go to his meetings."

I told him, "You will be making a mistake if you do that," and I related what had happened to the other pastor who had done the same thing.

"But," the pastor insisted, "if you don't forbid your people to go, some of them will go to his meetings."

"Sure they will go. But I'm not a dictator. Believers aren't under a dictatorship in the family of God. Besides, that minister is not in competition with me. I'm feeding my people the Word."

The pastor said, "Well, I'm going to forbid my people to go."

I said, "If you do that, every one of them will go just to see if it's as bad as you said it was. That's why I'm not even going to mention it to my congregation."

I knew that pastor was wrong, but I couldn't convince him. I never even mentioned to my congregation that the other minister was in town. However, finally there was so much controversy stirred up about that minister's meetings that people began asking me about them. Then I had to make a public statement about it because he was going to be running his meetings all summer long.

I said to my congregation, "Many have asked me about the tent meetings here in town. I don't agree with everything the fellow is preaching. But I would say that about ninety percent of what he is preaching is absolutely correct. A person can be right in his heart and wrong in his head. I think he is wrong on some things, yet God is blessing him. He is getting people saved and healed, so more power to him.

"People have asked me," I continued, "if they can attend his meetings. I'm not a dictator. We have services Sunday morning, Sunday night, and Wednesday night. When the doors are open, you should be faithful to your home church and be here. The rest of the time, go anywhere you want to go. Just eat the hay and leave the sticks."

Do you know, I never lost a church member! But when that other pastor commanded his congregation not to attend those meetings, he lost seven of the best families in his church. Actually, he almost lost his church, because those families were his staunchest financial supporters, and after they left, he couldn't even make the church payments.

Pastors are not to be dictators! Of course, if a minister is teaching doctrine that is harmful to people, then a pastor is obligated to warn his flock. But on the other hand, if a pastor just keeps feeding the people, they will keep coming back and not stray to other churches.

Governing the Local Body
Spiritually and Naturally

There is both the spiritual and the natural side to the word "governments" in First Corinthians 12:28. In other words, the pastor has the spiritual oversight of the church, but he also has to deal with the natural side of running a church. For example, pastors have to oversee the buying of property, building new buildings, buying equipment, and so forth. All of those things are accomplished in the natural realm.

Well, is the pastor to oversee all of that? Yes, to some extent. However, if he just spends all his time on things in the natural realm, he won't be ready to preach, nor will he have the *anointing* to preach! So he will have to maintain some balance in this area. I have seen some pastors spend so much of their time in the daily running of the church that the anointing to preach and teach the Word began to wane.

As his church grows and develops, the pastor needs to have enough wisdom to delegate some of the natural tasks and responsibilities. On the natural side of running a church, the pastor will not necessarily handle the finances of the church. But he needs to maintain some oversight in the financial area.

In other words, he can delegate that responsibility to someone else, but still needs to know what is going on financially in his church. Some pastors delegate all of the natural responsibilities to others and eventually lose their church because they do not know about or oversee any of the natural functions. There is a balance.

Also, just because a minister is a preacher doesn't necessarily mean he is a businessman or that he will have ability or expertise in natural tasks such as church building projects. Some pastors do and some pastors don't. But whether a pastor has natural ability or not, it would be wise for him to have some kind of advisory board to counsel him in the business matters of the church.

But by the word "governments," the Bible is saying that the pastor is the spiritual head of the local assembly. In the local church there is no higher *spiritual* authority than the pastor because he has the *spiritual* oversight of the local body.

We see an example of the natural tasks and responsibilities of running a church being delegated to others in the Early Church. These men who were chosen to assist in the natural affairs in the church were the first deacons.

> **ACTS 6:1-6**
> **1 And in those days, when the number of the disciples was multiplied, there arose a murmuring of the Grecians against the Hebrews, because their widows were neglected in the daily ministration.**
> **2 Then the twelve called the multitude of the disciples unto them, and said, It is not reason that we should leave the word of God, and serve tables.**
> **3 Wherefore, brethren, look ye out among you seven men of HONEST REPORT, FULL OF THE HOLY GHOST and WISDOM, whom we may APPOINT OVER THIS BUSINESS.**
> **4 But we will give ourselves continually to prayer, and to the ministry of the word.**
> **5 And the saying pleased the whole multitude: and they chose Stephen, a man full of faith and of the Holy Ghost, and Philip, and Prochorus, and Nicanor, and Timon, and Parmenas, and Nicolas a proselyte of Antioch:**
> **6 Whom they set before the apostles: and when they had prayed, they laid their hands on them.**

Remember, the apostles were the only ministers the

Early Church had to begin with, and at first the church at Jerusalem was the only local body in existence. But by the time this account in Acts 6 occurred, the local body at Jerusalem had grown large enough that it became necessary to choose men who could administer the business and the natural affairs of the church.

We know from the Scriptures that the Jerusalem church had grown to at least 8,120 members (Acts 1:15; 2:41; 4:4). Up until this time, the apostles had done all the work of the ministry; they had carried out both the *spiritual* and the *natural* tasks.

The Greek word "deacon" means an *attendant* or generally speaking, a *helper*. Because these deacons helped in the natural affairs of the church, it left the apostles free to preach and teach the Word of God.

In Acts 6:3, we can see the limits of the deacons' ministry: "*. . . men . . . whom we may appoint over this BUSINESS.*" Nowhere in the New Testament will you find deacon boards deciding *doctrine* of the church or having the *spiritual oversight* of the church. The apostles delegated the *natural* tasks and the *business* affairs of the church to this group of men, and these deacons were chosen on the basis of certain qualifications.

First, these deacons were chosen for their *honest reputation*. They had to be *full of the Holy Ghost*. But notice they were also required to have *wisdom*. If deacons, who are just helpers in the church, need to have an honest report and wisdom — how much more should preachers of the gospel!

The reason some preachers fail is that they don't have an honest report, and they lack wisdom in dealing with money. Or some ministers fail because they put people in positions of handling money who don't have an honest report or any practical wisdom in business affairs. That's unscriptural. People shouldn't handle money if they don't have an honest report or if they lack wisdom in financial affairs.

But here's another place where some pastors are missing it. Some pastors of small congregations put an administrator over the practical business affairs so they can give themselves to prayer and the Word. Then these pastors go to the other extreme and don't keep track of the business affairs of the church at all.

But if a pastor doesn't check up on the financial affairs of the church, his church could get in a mess financially, and he wouldn't even know it until it was too late. That's why a pastor needs to know what is going on financially in his church even if he has delegated the financial tasks to others.

I pastored smaller congregations of two or three hundred people, and I knew everything that was going on spiritually *and* financially in the church. At the same time I did a lot of praying, and I was in the Word continually. I didn't handle the money myself; I delegated that to someone else, but that person was accountable to me so I would know what was going on financially in the church.

Pastors and Church Boards

When I got the baptism in the Holy Ghost and came over among Pentecostal circles, I didn't know much in some of these areas. In every single church I pastored, I found out that the previous pastors had had trouble with their church boards.

I didn't think the church government was just exactly right in any one of the churches where I pastored. I knew from the Word that the pastor has the oversight of the local church both spiritually and naturally. Yet some of these church boards in these churches where I pastored wanted to run the church both naturally and spiritually.

Well, I didn't go to those churches to try to take over and change their church government. I came to preach the Word and to be a blessing to the people and to take care of the flock of God in that local church.

If I had gone into those churches with an attitude of trying to take over and changing everything overnight, I would have gotten things in a mess, and the board would have sent me on my way. And they would have been right in doing that. But I didn't take a dictatorial attitude. I went to those churches to help and bless the people and to work within their existing church structure.

For example, in the last church I pastored, we needed to build a church addition and redecorate the sanctuary. That's part of the natural side of running a church, isn't it? And it requires dealing with the business side of the ministry.

I had enough sense not to go to that church board that had been in existence long before I got there, and demand, "We're going to remodel this church the way *I* want it."

Instead, I asked them, "How do you want to remodel? After all, this is your church. After I'm gone, you'll still be here. So let's just consider the needs of the entire congregation when we remodel the sanctuary."

Every other pastor had had problems working with those same church boards. But I found out that the other pastors came in with the dictatorial attitude, *I want everyone to know I'm the pastor here. I'm running this church, and what I say goes! You do what I tell you!*

Dear Lord, a pastor with an attitude like that is going to run into trouble with any church board! A pastor shouldn't go to a church and just start trying to change everything. He should work with the existing church board and church government. If he can't do that, he shouldn't pastor that church.

I didn't have the trouble some pastors do with their church boards because I didn't have a dictatorial attitude. I didn't try to go into a church and take over and change everything all at once. As much as possible a pastor should try to work with existing church boards.

I remember one pastor who didn't do that. When this pastor took over a certain church, he decided he needed to totally change the church government. He told me personally, "God can't bless us because we don't have the correct church government. So I've got to institute a New Testament church government."

I tried to get him not to do that. I told him, "First of all, you haven't been there long enough to start trying to change things. In the second place, that church existed long before you got there so you're not going to be able to change things overnight. Pastor at least a year, and probably two years, without changing a thing in the church structure."

I said, "Just prove to the people that you love them. A good shepherd gives his life for the sheep. And once you prove to them that you love them and have their best interests at heart, they'll follow you anywhere God leads you."

He said, "But we just can't have God's blessings and the power of God in demonstration until we get the correct church government."

I said to him, "That's not true! I know better than that. I pastored nearly twelve years, and I'll be perfectly honest with you. None of the churches I pastored had what I considered 'correct' New Testament church government. But I didn't try to change a thing. And yet every church board told me, 'Since you've been here, we've experienced the greatest church growth and the greatest move of the Holy Spirit in the history of our church.'"

You see, what God does and how He manifests Himself in a church doesn't depend on church government — unless it has been taken completely out of the guidelines of New Testament doctrine. God is more interested in us walking in love and in unity with one another than He is in our having what we might technically consider to be the right structure.

I asked this pastor, "Is God blessing your church? Is anyone getting saved, healed, or baptized in the Holy Ghost?"

He said, "Yes, in nearly every service."

I answered, "Then it seems to me that God is blessing you."

Then he gave me *his* idea of correct church government. Do you know what it was? It was, "*I am the head, so I will handle all the money.*"

I said, "You'd better watch that. Don't do it."

I talked to him many times, but he wouldn't listen. I knew what was going to happen, and it did. After he changed the church government and instituted what he thought was the correct church government, it was amazing how God "blessed" them! When he first started pastoring that congregation, the membership was about 1,500 people. After he instituted his idea of "correct" church government, within eighteen months, he had less than 200 people.

He was too hardheaded to listen. He was about the same age I was when I pastored. One thing I can honestly say, as a young minister, I always listened to ministers who had more experience in the faith. Whether I agreed with them or not, I always took to heart what they said because I knew they were more seasoned in the ministry.

Some of them didn't know a thing in the world about the so-called faith message. But they knew a lot about some other things that helped and blessed me immeasurably. A person should have enough sense to stay teachable and listen to older ministers who have much experience in the ministry.

As a young minister, I understood the need to work with the existing church boards in the churches I pastored. Each of those churches were in existence before I came, so it wasn't *my* church. It's different if a pastor builds a church from the beginning and pioneers a new work.

If he starts a work of his own, he can do things the way he feels directed of the Lord. But even then, he will have to be careful that he walks in love and doesn't become a dictator. Even if he started the church, it is still not *his* church; it's the Lord's church. And he is still going to have to walk in love and put the people first.

Love always considers the other person first. When it came to the spiritual oversight of the church, these church boards understood that I was the head of the church and they never tried to tell me what to do. They honored me, and I honored them.

Some pastors also miss it with their church board because they say, "The Lord told me such and such, so we are going to do it this way!" I never said that to any church board, even if the Lord had told me something, because then that puts them under bondage to do what I've said.

For example, in one of the churches I pastored, we had a business meeting once a month. We would discuss money issues — property, insurance on buildings, and general church business affairs.

Brother Haynes was one of the board members, and whatever way he voted, the other two men on the board would follow him. I would let Brother Haynes say whatever he wanted to, and then if I knew the Lord was leading in another direction, I would say, "Let's try it this way, and if it proves to be wrong, we can change and do it your way."

That sounded reasonable, so they all agreed to it. After nine months, Brother Haynes said, "Men, Brother Hagin has been here nine months, and he's never suggested anything that didn't work out well. Let's just go on record right now that whatever he wants to do, we'll follow him."

My suggestions worked out because I had sought God about the situations, and I had the mind of the Lord on what we were to do. I didn't necessarily tell the church board that, but I proved myself, so they trusted me. They saw that I loved them and had their best interests at heart. When a church board gains confidence in a pastor, they are usually willing to work with him and implement his ideas.

I gained their trust, so they supported me in whatever I wanted to do. They knew I wouldn't take advantage of them. I lived right and did right in front of them, and they knew they could trust me.

But some time after I left that church, they got another pastor. The church had seven different charitable funds to help people, including a missionary fund, a hospital fund, and a building fund. The church board turned all the finances of the church over to the new pastor, and he stole every dime they had.

One of the church deacons told me, "We could have put him in jail, but we didn't want to advertise that a Full Gospel pastor had been arrested for embezzlement."

That pastor knew the church board wouldn't prosecute him because it would create a scandal for the church, and he took advantage of that. A fellow like that is a crook. Talk about false pastors — that man was a false pastor! A man like that is no more a pastor than these fellows who claim to be apostles and prophets and want to rule over everyone so churches will tithe to them.

You see, a church board can sometimes run into this kind of unhappy dilemma in the practical side of running a church. On the one side, to keep from being swindled, a church may have to make some strict bylaws and rules, which can tie a pastor's hands so it's hard for him to accomplish anything. But on the other hand, if a church just turns all the financial matters over to a new pastor without any checks and balances, some unscrupulous fellow could come along like that man and steal every dime they have.

So although there are some guidelines about church government, there are no ironclad rules. I've just always operated on what the Bible says, ". . . *Provide things honest in the sight of all men*" (Rom. 12:17). If a pastor is endeavoring to walk with the Lord, and his heart is right with God, he doesn't want to take advantage of people. He wants to bless them and give his life for the sheep.

Chapter 13
Different Church Structures

Different kinds of church structures have evolved in different denominations. People ask, "Which kind of church government is right?" Actually, there are certain truths and benefits to each one of them. And sometimes I think God blesses us not *because* of our church structures, but *in spite* of them.

In one particular church organization, for example, the district supervisors of the denomination choose the shepherds for their churches. They base that on the principle that sheep in a flock don't vote on who their shepherd should be. Therefore, they reason that only the district supervisors or overseers of the sheep are qualified to select a shepherd for the sheep of a local body.

That system seems to work fine for them. Their fundamentals of doctrine are scriptural, so God can bless them. And they have experienced substantial church growth.

In another leading organization, the congregation elects and votes on the pastor. They also experience the blessings of God in their denomination. People are continually saved, healed, and filled with the Holy Spirit.

Another organization has chosen a combination of the two types of church government. Their district supervisor meets with the board, and he suggests who he feels the Lord is directing to be the next pastor. Then they all pray about it and bring it before the church congregation to vote on.

One district supervisor of this particular denomination told me, "I always say to the congregation, 'You understand that you don't have to accept this pastor if you don't think it is the will of God for this church. But I have prayed about it, the board has prayed about it, and now you pray about it.'"

Which church government is right? They all have their benefits. But the point is that a pastor will have to work within the framework of the existing church government where he is pastoring. He needs to stay with their structure and not try to change it.

I attended a General Council of a certain denomination in 1951. The General Secretary of that denomination said some things about church government that were helpful to me.

He said, "When I first began pastoring, my church was the only Full Gospel church in town, and I had preached to my congregation that organization was wrong and sinful. But in the process of time, I saw the need for some kind of organization or church government."

So this minister sent out letters to various ministers, and as a result, he founded a leading denomination.

"But," he said, "I had taught my people that organization was wrong, so when we began to organize, I lost half my church! They said to me, 'You've compromised! The devil got ahold of you. God can't bless you with that compromising spirit.' And they went across town and founded an independent work."

This pastor said, "When half of my church members went across town and founded an independent work, they called us renegades and said God couldn't bless us because we were operating within the framework of an organized church government. They claimed, 'God *can* bless *us* because we're independent. We're not bound by anything.'

"But," the pastor continued, "two or three years went by, and to my utter astonishment, that other church grew about as much as we did. Both of our congregations doubled. We reached out to the unsaved, and so did they. And God blessed us both."

"Finally, after about five years, that other pastor came to me and said, 'God have mercy on both of us! I've been watching your church. I was sure God couldn't bless you because you had organized, but He's blessed you and you've grown. And God has blessed us and we've grown. Let's just forget about our differences. We'll keep our church government, and you keep yours, but let's fellowship with one another.'"

The pastor said, "So I began to preach in his church, and he began to come to my church and preach. I found out that God wasn't so concerned about our different church governments as we thought He was. He blessed us both in spite of our differences."

'Who Is an Elder?'

In my hometown when I was a boy, one of the

churches split over the question, "Who is an elder?" and "What constitutes the office of an elder?" One group left the church and built another church, and they chose businessmen to be elders to run the church. They thought that was correct church government.

They started out with a congregation of more than one hundred people, and after several years, five people were left in the congregation!

You see, businessmen don't have the anointing on them to stand in the pastoral office. An ordained minister — a man who was called to the pastoral office — pastored the other church in town. That church kept growing until they outgrew their facilities and had to build a new church building. That kind of growth says something about correct church government!

When Paul addresses *elders* or *pastors* in Acts 20:28, he is talking about people who are called to the pastoral office. Preachers and teachers of the Word are spiritually equipped to feed the flock of God the Word. These elders were not businessmen who were put in charge of the church.

It is unscriptural to put businessmen who are neither called or anointed as spiritual overseers in a local body, or to have a board of elders made up of businessmen. In terms of the local church, an *elder* is a *pastor* — a preacher or teacher of the Word — not a businessman who has been appointed to be an elder in the church.

Businessmen can be helpers or deacons, and very often their financial and business expertise can be a great assistance to the pastor. But businessmen have no anointing on them to stand in the pastoral office. They have no anointing on them to spiritually oversee the church of God, nor do they have an anointing to feed the flock of God with the Word.

Only someone who is equipped by the Holy Spirit to stand in a ministry office — the pastoral office — can be an elder (in the spiritual sense of the term), an overseer, or a bishop. A businessman doesn't have the anointing or the spiritual equipment to stand in a ministry office.

You see, scripturally speaking, every pastor is an elder. Actually, every ordained minister is an elder, whether he is an apostle, prophet, evangelist, pastor, or teacher. Eldership is not a separate office from the five-fold ministry.

That's the reason the Bible teaches that we are not to take a novice and put him in an office of authority or in a ministry office. We are to wait until he proves his ministry and gains some spiritual maturity and experience before he is ordained to full eldership in the Body of Christ.

It's important that ministers should reach a certain age, maturity, and experience in ministry before they are ordained, because ordination is the act of officially recognizing that a minister has attained to full eldership in the Body of Christ. Eldership is not for those just starting out in ministry or for spiritual novices.

Of course, people can buy ordinations from fly-by-night organizations. Many do that and call themselves "ministers." But that doesn't make them ordained ministers of the gospel! They are just spiritual babies playing church. No, ministers and ministries must first be proved. And ministers need to study to show themselves approved (1 Tim. 3:10; 2 Tim. 2:15). Also, the Bible gives certain qualifications for ministers (1 Tim. 3:1-13; Titus 1:6-9).

So the apostle, prophet, teacher, and evangelist are all elders in the Body of Christ because they are ordained to the full-time ministry. And a pastor is most certainly an elder in the Body of Christ because he shepherds the local flock.

Plurality of Elders

People have fought small wars on the subject of eldership and church government. Some teach that a plurality of elders — a board of elders — must govern the church in order for it to be a true New Testament church.

But nowhere in the scriptures do you find a structure where a board of elders dominates the local church and tells the pastor and the congregation what to do. That kind of structure is not in the Scriptures.

Some people ask the question, Is a *plurality* of elders scripturally correct? It depends on what they mean by that. If by a plurality of elders they mean that several ministers of equal authority should run a church, the answer is no. Anything with two or more heads is a freak. You couldn't have five elders or pastors with equal authority running one church! It would be impossible.

But if by plurality of elders, people mean that the senior pastor is the overseer of the church, and he has associate or assistant pastors helping him, the answer is yes, that is scriptural. That is not a leadership having two heads, but it is a plurality of eldership. The associate pastors have their input, but the senior pastor makes the final decision. Someone has to be the main shepherd of the local church.

If a pastor has a small congregation, he can usually take care of the people, and he doesn't really need any more elders or associates to help him. But the pastor ought to have enough sense to know when he needs associates to help take care of the flock.

Some churches call their associate pastors *elders*. Others call them pastors, shepherds, or bishops. We have Scripture for all those terms. God may even raise up someone from a pastor's own congregation to help him, who is called to the fivefold ministry and is a faithful worker in the church. However, he cannot be a novice in spiritual things.

Some people teach that the Early Church had a plurality of elders as their church government. They cite the passage in Acts 20:17 where Paul addressed the elders at the church of Ephesus as an example of plurality of eldership.

But, you see, that church was the only church they had in Ephesus at that time. There could have been many members in the church by then, and it may have taken more than one person to oversee it.

The same thing was true of the mother church in

Jerusalem. When you talk about plurality of elders running a church, you have to take into consideration that the church in Jerusalem was the only local body to begin with, and it was a large church.

It would certainly take more than one pastor to oversee all those people, wouldn't it? They had to have a plurality of elders to adequately minister to all the people.

We do the same thing today in our larger churches, although we don't necessarily call them "elders." We call them assistants or associates. But in a small church of a couple hundred people, a plurality of elders is not usually necessary.

Let me give you an example of the development of a plurality of elders in a local church. RHEMA Bible Church has been formally registered as a church since 1976. I taught there occasionally, as would others. But in 1985 we began the church with a full schedule of services, and my son, Kenneth Hagin Jr., officially became the pastor.

As the pastor, Ken is the head of the church; I'm not. He is my pastor. Even though I stand in the offices of the prophet and teacher, I don't have a thing in the world to do with running RHEMA Bible Church; I'm not part of the pastoral staff, nor do I help govern the church. I just sit on the pew with everyone else and enjoy the services.

When RHEMA Bible Church began, Ken had three associate pastors, a youth minister, and a minister of music. As the church grew and developed, Ken added a children's minister to the church staff. That is a true plurality of elders. But we don't call it that; we call them associate pastors. The church is continually growing in numbers so that associate pastors were and are necessary to adequately minister to all the people.

On the other hand, when I pastored country churches, I really didn't need an associate. But when I did need help occasionally, I'd get someone else to help me. That didn't mean that person was supposed to come in and run things; he was there to assist me. But I wasn't a dictator either. A pastor shouldn't take a dictatorial view in running the local body because then he's not walking in love.

What I'm trying to point out is that in many local churches today that have a pastoral staff, a plurality of elders has been functioning all the time. We've not called them "elders" even though that is their function in the local church. We've just called them associate pastors.

False Pastors and Ministers

Yes, there are false pastors and false ministers. A *false* minister is someone who is trying to operate in an office when he is not called to that office. Anyone who is in the ministry for personal gain and doesn't have the people at heart is false. There are false pastors, just as there are false prophets and false apostles — or any other ministry gift for that matter.

False pastors are those in the pastoral ministry who are either not called to that office at all or who are putting themselves and their own interests before the needs of the sheep. A false pastor is also one who teaches things that hurt and divide his flock.

A good shepherd would rather die than see a church split or hurt in any way. But I have known some so-called pastors, especially years ago, who caused problems in every church they pastored. They put themselves before the people.

A person who does that doesn't have a shepherd's heart. A good shepherd puts the people before his own interests and desires, and he will sacrifice and give his life for the sheep, including protecting his congregation from false ministers and false teaching.

That's why a pastor needs to be careful about those whom he invites to preach in his pulpit. A pastor won't necessarily agree on everything of minor importance that other ministers preach. But there are extreme doctrines that tear up churches and hurt innocent people.

That's why a pastor should check up on ministers and find out what a fellow is preaching before inviting a minister to preach in his church. And he shouldn't just believe everything a traveling minister tells him about his accomplishments in the ministry either.

A pastor should see what effect traveling ministers have had on churches where they have preached — whether it has been positive or negative. Has a traveling minister been a blessing in churches where he has ministered? Or has he caused division and strife wherever he has preached? If ministers have torn up other churches doctrinally in the past, they are liable to leave a trail of churches in the same mess.

We need to remember that Paul exposed false ministers for the sake of the Body of Christ. He said, *"Now I beseech you, brethren, mark them which cause divisions and offences contrary to the doctrine which ye have learned; and avoid them"* (Rom. 16:17).

You see, we are not talking about exposing individual ministers just to hurt and damage their reputations. But a pastor has to be concerned with *issues* and sound biblical *doctrine*. He needs to protect his flock, and sometimes for the sake of his flock, he will have to expose error if it is dividing and hurting the local body.

One error a pastor needs to guard his flock against is these so-called prophets that seem to be cropping up in the church today. What is a false prophet? For one thing, it refers to any so-called prophet who would go into a pastor's church and publicly prophesy to him in such a way as to embarrass him and divide his church. Prophecies that divide a church and embarrass a pastor aren't from God!

In our day, we sometimes hear of so-called prophets going into a church and publicly prophesying to the pastor, "God shows me that He's through with you here. You are suppose to leave this church!"

Anyone who would publicly prophesy the pastor right out of the pulpit and divide and hurt his church, is a false prophet. That is not only unscriptural and asinine, it is lying. Any so-called prophet who says things like that needs to quit lying on God. God would never tell anyone to embarrass a pastor right in front of his own congregation and hurt and confuse the sheep!

You see, there is just a fine line between fanaticism and true spirituality. That's why traveling ministers need to exercise a great deal of wisdom and discretion when they go into someone's church. Traveling ministers may know some things in the Spirit, but that doesn't mean they're supposed to go around broadcasting what they know.

My wife and I visited a certain church, in which one of our own RMAI people was the pastor. (RMAI is the name for our ministerial association, RHEMA Ministerial Association International.) A day or two after we visited the church, I said to my wife, "Could you sense that God has something else for the pastor to do, and that it is time for him to leave the church?" She agreed that she had sensed that in her spirit too.

But we didn't call the church together and prophesy that in front of everyone. Nor did we get the pastor's church board together and embarrass him by telling the board that he was supposed to leave the church. We talked to him privately.

Even then we didn't say, "We have a word from God for you." We very gently suggested, "It would be good to pray and seek the Lord, because we sensed in our spirits that God has some things for you."

After that he began to pray and seek God, and he called us later and told us, "God told me it's time to leave the church. He has other things for me to do."

By trying to deal with something publicly that should

have been done privately, we could have created great damage in that church, divided it, and messed up the plan of God for that local body.

Usually ministers who cause trouble and divide churches are those who take the attitude, *No one is going to tell me what to do!* Or, *No one is going to tell me what to preach about!* But if a minister can't be a blessing to a congregation, he doesn't have any business preaching.

Chapter 14
Ministerial Accountability

Every minister ought to be accountable to someone because the Bible says, *"For none of us liveth to himself, and no man dieth to himself"* (Rom. 14:7). Actually, there isn't any such thing as an *independent* work or an *independent* minister. We are all dependent on one another because we are all members of the same body (Rom. 12:5; 1 Cor. 12:12). We need one another.

If a minister calls himself an "independent" minister, at the very least from a spiritual standpoint he ought to be answerable to the home church he came out of. Or if he belongs to a ministerial fellowship, he needs to be answerable to them.

The pastor is the spiritual head of the local church; therefore, the traveling minister is accountable to that pastor while he is ministering in that particular church. And then it is also true that the pastor ought to be accountable to someone. First of all, of course, in matters of ministerial ethics and integrity, a pastor is accountable to the congregation he oversees.

But ministers, including pastors, should belong to some kind of fellowship, where they can receive input into their lives and ministries and operate with some kind of accountability. Ministerial fellowships should help ministers, not seek to control them, but to be a blessing to them.

So if a minister is a member of an organization, he should be accountable to that organization. If a minister calls himself an "independent" minister and doesn't belong to some kind of a ministerial fellowship, at the least he needs to be accountable to the home church he came out of. The Bible says, ". . . *in multitude of counsellors there is safety*" (Prov. 24:6).

Actually, in the Acts of the Apostles, when a question arose about doctrine, the disciples went back to their home church, which was the church at Jerusalem (*see* Acts 15).

Every pastor needs a pastor and a home church from which he himself can periodically receive ministry. In other words, we all need one another. Ministers need to hear the preaching and teaching of God's Word, too, just as their congregations do. And sometimes ministers need to be corrected spiritually, just as their congregations need to be corrected spiritually.

Some ministers have lost their churches or are out of the ministry today because they wouldn't listen to godly counsel from seasoned ministers. In some cases, if they had listened to someone who was spiritually experienced, they would still be in the ministry.

Sometimes ministers have called me and asked my advice about something they were planning to do in ministry. Sometimes I've advised them, "Don't do that because it will hurt your ministry." But some of them didn't listen. I knew what they wanted to do was neither scriptural nor wise, but they did it anyway. In some instances, they made shipwreck of their ministries and are not in the ministry today.

Sometimes people have taught doctrine we don't endorse, but they claim to be a part of RHEMA. They may have gone out from us, and at one time may have been scripturally correct in doctrine. But we don't endorse the doctrinal error that some are now teaching.

Yes, we ought to be for unity in the Body of Christ, whether we are members of the same local congregation or not because the Body of Christ is one. We can get into trouble by not walking in love toward fellow members of the Body of Christ.

But on the other hand, Paul himself said, *". . . mark them which cause divisions and offences contrary to the doctrine which ye have learned; and avoid them"* (Rom. 16:17). Paul said to mark those who are causing trouble, division, and strife in the Body of Christ and not to have anything to do with them.

Actually, in some cases that *is* walking in love. If you didn't mark them and hold them accountable for their sin or doctrinal error, they might never be led to repentance and could do a great deal of damage to the Body of Christ. You have to ask yourself, *What would love do?* In some cases, the greatest demonstration of love is to expose doctrinal error and protect other members of the Body of Christ from extreme teaching.

When your little children played with matches, the first time you probably reprimanded them and told them about the danger of fire. If you caught them playing with matches again, you probably gave them a swat and told them to stop it. But if you caught them playing with matches the third time, you probably gave them a good spanking so they would remember it.

Were you acting in love? Of course you were. You may have saved their lives because they could have caught the house on fire. It's the same way in the Body of Christ. Yes, you want to act in love, but there is another side of love too. Jesus was a Man of love and power when He walked upon this earth, yet in righteous indignation, He drove the money changers out of the temple (John 2:13-17).

Ministerial Restoration

Because the local church is like a family, you will have some of the same problems in a church that you have in a family. Children need to be disciplined, and sometimes church members need to be disciplined or corrected.

But the same thing is true concerning pastors and ministers. Sometimes ministers experience problems — moral, financial, and even doctrinal problems — just as other people can have various problems. Sometimes they need discipline and correction. And we need to help them when we can.

Years ago I asked a leader of a certain denomination, "When ministers miss it and fail, why isn't it handled biblically? The Bible says in Galatians 6:1, '... *if a man be overtaken in a fault, ye which are spiritual, restore such an one in the spirit of meekness; considering thyself, lest thou also be tempted.*' Why aren't ministers restored like the Bible instructs?"

He said, "Brother Hagin, I believe many men who stumble and sin could be restored. If folks want to repent and do right, they ought to be helped. Of course, if they won't listen and won't take biblical counsel, a ministerial association wouldn't have any choice; they would have to revoke their credentials."

I was concerned about this, because I knew that some ministers who failed and made a mistake could have been restored. Some of them never did get back in the ministry because when they missed it, their denomination publicized it, and their reputations were ruined.

Then when everyone knew about their problem, these ministers were told, "*Now* go prove yourself!" But after their downfall was publicized, no one would fellowship with them! And pastors wouldn't allow them to preach in their churches, so the majority of them never got back into the ministry.

Why don't we restore and recover ministers who have made a mistake? Of course, if they don't want to be recovered and don't want to live uprightly before God, that's a different thing entirely. But I'm talking about ministers who want to repent and do what's right.

In Galatians 6:1, the Bible says, "consider yourself, lest you also be tempted." After all, in the same circumstances, some of us might not have done as well as some of them did. But we are so quick to criticize and judge others.

I was concerned about this, so I went to the Lord in prayer about it. I said, "Lord, Your Word says, '. . . *if a man be overtaken in a fault, ye which are spiritual,*

restore such an one in the spirit of meekness. . . .' I said,
"Lord, it doesn't say to *destroy* ministers who miss it by
broadcasting their problem; it says to *restore* them.
Why don't we restore them?"

The Lord answered and said, "Your answer is in that
verse."

I didn't see what He was talking about. I said to Him
again, "Lord, why don't we *restore* ministers who stumble and fall?"

He said, "Your answer is in that verse. Read it
again."

I read it again, but I still didn't see it. I asked the
Lord the third time, and again He said, "Your answer is
in that verse. Read it again."

I said, "Well, if it is, I can't see it."

Then again I read, ". . . *ye which are SPIRITUAL. . . .*"
I saw it! The Bible is saying, "If there are any spiritual
people among you, they would *restore* those who have
fallen — not judge, criticize, or destroy them."

I said to the Lord, "Oh! I got my answer."

One denomination deals with restoring fallen ministers in a way I feel is most scriptural. For example,
years ago one of their ministers got into moral difficulty
with one of the women in the church. He was married
and so was the woman. They both repented and wanted
to walk right before the Lord.

The supervisor of the district came to counsel the
minister and told him, "It would be good for you to
change churches. We are not going to publicize this to
anyone because you've repented and straightened it all

out among yourselves. We are going to restore you, but it would be good for you to move to another state, and we will give you an opportunity to prove yourself."

So after a time of restoration, they gave the minister another church to pastor in another state, and they didn't publicize that he had fallen. But they told the supervisor in that other state about the minister's problem, so he could be of help to this minister. They practiced this scripture and restored the man, and they put him in a situation where he *could* prove himself.

However, this particular minister did the same thing again; he had an affair with a woman in that church too. The district supervisor went to him the second time and gave him a period of time to restore himself spiritually and make restitution.

But this time he told the minister, "We will give you one more chance. But if you get into any moral difficulty the third time, we won't restore you to the pastorate again. You will be immediately dismissed, and you can never renew your papers with us."

The Body of Christ shouldn't publicize everything that happens within its ranks. Things like this shouldn't be brought out in the public. Those of us in the Church should have enough spirituality to deal with these things privately within the confines of the Church.

When something happens in your family, do you go out and broadcast it? No. In the same way, the Church is a family. We ought to have enough sense to know how to deal with some of these problems in the Church and help people so their lives can be restored, not ruined, and they can learn how to be a blessing to the Body of Christ.

I know one minister who was used mightily of God years ago. He got into moral trouble, and the superintendent of that denomination told me, "This man's wife admitted to me that she was to blame for it. She admitted she had never been a wife to him, and it caused her husband to stumble. But she repented, and their marriage was restored."

That man's ministry was also restored, and he had a fruitful ministry. You see, we ought to save people if we can. The Body of Christ should be in the saving business — restoring folks — not destroying them. You understand it's a different thing entirely if people don't want to repent and do what is right. If they want to keep on doing wrong, they will need to be dealt with scripturally.

We do see accountability in the New Testament (1 Cor. 5:5). And following the New Testament pattern, those disciples who went out from the Jerusalem church were accountable to that church (Acts 15:1-23).

In other words, traveling ministers answered to a local congregation. And if there was a problem, they would go back to the home church they came out of for advice or to settle issues of doctrine (*see* Acts 15). The disciples answered to the church they had come out of as opposed to an outside board or congregation.

Financial Accountability

Every minister needs to be financially accountable to

someone. For example, at RHEMA, we have a board of advisors who are successful businessmen. They advise us on natural affairs; we seek their advice on business matters. Ministers should not think they are above taking advice, especially when they can consult someone with expertise in an area.

We are accountable to our board of advisors in the business affairs of RHEMA. In fact, they are the ones who set our salaries. Then they give us the authority to set the salaries for our employees.

Once a year, we have an all-day business meeting, and these businessmen examine our financial reports. All of our books are also audited, of course, by a professional firm. But we are also accountable in business matters to this board of advisors as well. That is scriptural because the Bible says, ". . . *Provide things honest in the sight of all men*" (Rom. 12:17).

A smaller church or ministry may operate differently, but every minister should be accountable in some way for the handling of church funds if he is to be in line with Scripture.

You see, that's the natural side of the ministry. But that board of advisors doesn't have anything to do with the spiritual oversight of running the church or the ministry. They only advise us in business matters. The pastor has the *spiritual* oversight of the church. And there is no higher authority in the local body than the pastoral office.

However, even in spiritual things, if a pastor needs advice, he ought to have enough sense to go to those who are of sound biblical reputation like Paul did and get their advice, lest he run his spiritual race in vain (Gal. 2:2).

Ministerial Ethics and Etiquette

One of the first things to keep in mind about ministerial ethics is to simply practice the Golden Rule: Do unto others as you would have them do unto you.

Ministers of the gospel always need to keep in mind that they are children of their Heavenly Father, who is a God of love. The love of God has been shed abroad in our hearts by the Holy Ghost (Rom. 5:5). But even ministers have to allow their hearts to dominate them in dealing with people and others in the ministry.

If ministers walk in love toward fellow ministers and fellow Christians, then they are walking in the light of the Word of God. A minister can fulfill the plan, will, and purpose of God for his life as long as he walks in the light of God's Word and will.

Walking in love toward fellow ministers includes practicing ministerial etiquette. Pastors and traveling ministers need to realize they are laborers *together* in the Lord's harvest — not laborers *apart*.

I pastored for nearly twelve years. I'm so glad God gave me the glorious privilege to pastor. I sometimes think that every teacher, prophet, and evangelist on the field ought to pastor at least two or three years. They would learn invaluable lessons in dealing with people by pastoring. They would also not be so likely to come into a church with the unbiblical teachings and actions some of them preach and demonstrate.

Then, too, I sometimes think every pastor would benefit from being on the field for two or three years. Then he would learn how to treat traveling ministers when they come to his church.

But when a traveling minister does come into a pastor's church, he needs to realize that he is a guest in that church; he can't just come in and take over and do whatever *he* wants to.

Going into another man's church and trying to take over and do things his own way is like going into another man's home and trying to take over. A person wouldn't think of doing that in the natural, so why would he try to do that in the spiritual realm in a local church?

You see, I don't have the authority to come into your house and say, "I don't like this bedroom suite. I'm going to throw it out! And I don't like this dining room table either. I'm going to chop it up for firewood."

The same principle holds true in the house of God. I don't have any right to come into the house of God — into another man's church — and try to take over and do things my way. The pastor is the one in authority in the local church.

A pastor wrote me one time, telling me about his church. He had about two hundred people in his congregation. Another minister decided that he was an apostle, so he came to the pastor and said, "I'm an apostle now. God showed me that your church is one of *my* churches, and that I am to oversee it. Since I am an apostle, I can come in anytime I want to and take your pulpit over and preach as I see fit."

That's not only unethical; that's not scriptural! I would send a scoundrel like that down the road in an attitude of love! Could I do that in love? Let me ask you this: Did Jesus act in love when he took a whip and drove the money changers out of the temple (John 2:14-17)? He said to them, ". . . *It is written, My house is the house of prayer: but ye have made it a den of thieves"* (Luke 19:46). Of course it was. Jesus was a Man of love.

Some of these so-called apostles try to take over a pastor's church so they can take up an offering for themselves. Anyone who does that is a robber and a thief anyway. After all, they didn't start the church; the pastor is the one who labored in the ministry for that local body. He may have even started the work. He shouldn't allow anyone to come in and take over his church.

I'm for pastors! I believe in the local church. Pastors shouldn't pay any attention to people who don't believe in the local church and aren't committed to a local body themselves, or who come in and try to take over their churches.

This particular pastor told that fellow, "No, you can't take over my pulpit. You can come to the service if you want to, but you're going to sit in the pew just like everyone else. I'm the pastor here."

Too many people today are putting pastors down and trying to run roughshod over them. I read a transcript about what a certain so-called apostle taught. When this fellow got through talking about pastors, he had belittled the pastoral office to such a degree that you would have thought a pastor was worse than a old polecat!

But that's not what the Bible says. The Bible says, *"This is a true saying, If a man desire the office of a bishop, he desireth a GOOD work"* (1 Tim. 3:1). The Bible says the office of a bishop or pastor is a *good work*.

This so-called apostle taught that because the word "pastor" is only found one time in the New Testament, (and that is technically correct in the King James translation), therefore, it must not be a very important office.

But that so-called apostle didn't do his homework, because the pastoral office is referred to again and again in Scripture. As I've said, it is found in the words — *bishop, overseer, pastor, shepherd,* and *elder*. These all indicate the same office — the pastoral office. Actually, "elder" also signifies those called to the five-fold ministry. Every ordained minister is an elder.

But beware of those folks who leave a trail behind them of churches they have divided and split and where they've caused strife and dissension. I wouldn't have them in my church. That doesn't mean you are opposed to them personally. You may love them just as much as you ever did. But you're opposed to error because their fruit is not scripturally sound.

Another area where traveling ministers need to have wisdom and ministerial etiquette is in knowing what is appropriate to deal with publicly and what areas of ministry should be handled privately.

In all my years of ministry, I have very seldom dealt

with people's personal problems publicly. Some of these fellows who are going around revealing private matters, dealing with people's personal problems publicly, are out of order. And they need to be set in order by the pastor of the local congregation.

I've always made it a practice, even when I felt the Lord wanted me to minister specifically to an individual in a personal area, to first of all involve the pastor and obtain his permission. And, secondly, I've endeavored to minister discreetly so as to avoid bringing embarrassment to the person.

When I preach in another man's church, I get the pastor's permission before I deal with any sensitive issues involving individual members of his congregation. I don't have any business ministering privately or personally to another fellow's sheep about delicate issues without his permission. Any fellow who does that is a scoundrel.

Any preacher who comes into a pastor's church and tries to minister to someone else's sheep without the pastor's permission is out of line and out of order. He is a scoundrel. He needs prayer. Twelve grown men should take him twelve miles out into the country, and pray for him for twelve hours!

As a traveling minister, as I proved myself to be responsible in ministering in the local body, then pastors were always very gracious in giving me their full confidence to minister to their flock. I proved my ministry by acting in discretion and wisdom.

Ministerial Discretion

God doesn't put novices in positions of authority. One

reason He doesn't is that it takes time to become seasoned in the ministry and learn how to deal with situations in wisdom. A novice can get things in a mess if he doesn't know how to minister with discretion and wisdom in some of these areas.

For example, a traveling minister needs to know how to minister discreetly when going into another man's church. Prophets must above all be discreet in the things the Lord reveals to them about others.

I held a meeting at a certain pastor's church, and after the service I had a healing line. A young woman came forward for prayer. As soon as I began to pray for her, I knew exactly what was wrong with her. I also knew that her marriage was about to break up and why it was about to break up.

But this was a private matter, so I didn't deal with it publicly. A prophet, or any traveling minister for that matter, needs to be careful because he shouldn't always speak out everything he hears and sees in the spirit. By doing so, he can embarrass the person he's ministering to, the pastor, and even the congregation.

Besides, the prophet is a guest in that pastor's church, and as a guest, he needs to submit himself to the pastor because there is no higher authority in the local body than the pastoral office. In this instance, even though I knew by a revelation of the Holy Spirit what was wrong with this woman, I went to the pastor first and told him what I saw.

I told him, "I know this young woman's marriage is about to break up, and I know exactly why it's about to break up. But I won't deal with this situation without your permission."

You see, even though the Lord had revealed something to me supernaturally through the office of the prophet by the revelation gifts of the Spirit, I would never deal with another man's sheep without his permission. Prophets need to exercise some discretion, common sense, and ministerial ethics in these types of matters.

The pastor told me, "My wife and I have counseled her, trying to help her. If you can help this woman and her husband, I want you to do it." The pastor, his wife, and I ministered to that woman privately, and she was totally set free.

Traveling ministers who don't submit their ministries to the pastor of the local church where they are preaching are in error. For example, I've heard about some so-called prophets going into another man's church, and in front of the congregation take the service over and say, "I'm going to cast the devil out of So-and-so!"

The prophet doesn't have the right to do that without the pastor's permission. And usually it isn't a demon problem at all. Even if it is, it's not necessarily wise to deal with that publicly when there are baby Christians in the congregation who wouldn't understand.

But the point is, traveling ministers have no business dealing personally with another man's sheep without the pastor's permission. After all, the pastor is the shepherd of the local body, and he is responsible for that congregation. And visiting ministers shouldn't just go around trying to deal with some of these issues publicly in the first place. Ministers need discretion and wisdom in dealing with people in the local assembly.

I could tell you of experience after experience like that. Each time, even though I was standing in the office of the prophet and knew things by supernatural revelation of the Holy Spirit, I didn't usurp authority over the pastor.

No traveling minister, including the prophet, is above the pastor in the local body. That pastor is still the overseer in his own church; he's responsible for the sheep. As a guest in that church, the prophet is not the one in authority; the pastor is. Any traveling minister needs to submit his ministry to the pastor of the local assembly where he is ministering. That's not only ethical and proper, it's good ministerial etiquette.

Some people say, "Well, someone's got to preach and teach the truth!"

A traveling minister may be preaching the truth of God's Word. But the pastor may know that his congregation isn't ready to hear a particular teaching, even though it may be thoroughly scriptural. Certain teachings could do more harm than good if a congregation isn't spiritually mature. It could even split the church.

That pastor is there with those people all the time. If he is a true shepherd, he knows his people. Or he may know the people have had much teaching along a particular line, and that they need teaching on a different subject to balance their spiritual diet. The traveling minister won't necessarily know that.

There is a correlation between the natural realm and the spiritual realm. For example, in the natural, you can't feed a baby a beef steak or he would die. The same thing is true spiritually. And it's the pastor's responsibility to make sure his congregation is fed the proper spiritual diet.

No traveling minister should be a church splitter. He should edify and bless the local body. And even though prophets are equipped with spiritual gifts, they need to learn the purpose of them and how to use them constructively and with discretion. If prophets have any wisdom, they won't go around revealing everything they see and hear in the Spirit.

Any traveling minister, including a prophet, ought to be gentleman enough — and Christian enough — to tell the pastor ahead of time, "Correct me if I'm wrong." It's not right that innocent sheep are hurt because some traveling ministers don't minister with discretion and wisdom.

Over the years, I've told every pastor I've preached for, "You are the head of this local body, not me. Jesus is the Head of the Church, but you are an undershepherd. If I teach on any subject you don't want me to teach on, just tell me, and I will avoid that subject. Or if you see me do anything you don't want me to do, just tell me, and I won't do it anymore." That's where true submission comes in, dear friends.

Some of those pastors gave me marvelous advice and in some cases, sound constructive criticism. It wasn't destructive; it didn't destroy me. It greatly benefited me, and helped me change in some areas. Those pastors

had the same Holy Spirit I have. And the Word teaches
that we are laborers together, not laborers apart: *"For
we are labourers together with God . . ."* (1 Cor. 3:9).
That means we can learn from one another.

If a prophet's ministry is properly submitted to the
pastor of the local body, there may be times the Lord
will reveal something to the prophet that will greatly
help and benefit the local body. A pastor can trust a
proven, spiritually submitted ministry.

Of course, a prophet doesn't just speak out and
reveal everything he sees and hears. In fact, very seldom do I ever speak these things out. I usually deal
with the person personally; I don't call them up and
deal with them publicly in front of the whole crowd. A
prophet must be careful so he doesn't unnecessarily
embarrass anyone.

When I was out in field ministry, I always submitted
my ministry to the pastor of the church where I was
ministering. And I was always welcome to come back to
every church because I didn't leave churches in a mess.
I know ministers who cannot go back to churches where
they have ministered because of the trouble they
caused doctrinally and the strife and confusion they
stirred up. That's why a traveling minister needs to
submit his ministry to the local pastor.

Much difficulty has been caused in the Body of
Christ by false pastors, false apostles, and false
prophets. Churches have been torn up and have lost
members over unbiblical teaching in this area.

Any true minister of the gospel, no matter what

office he stands in, comes to bless the people, the church, and the community. If a minister comes to a church for his own personal gain, or to stir up strife and confusion, then he is a false minister of the gospel.

'I'm Not a Sheep Thief!'

There is another area of ministerial ethics and etiquette concerning the pastoral office. And that is in the area of stealing other pastors' sheep.

One church I pastored in east Texas had other neighboring churches close by. Three families that lived near my parsonage attended these other churches.

These other churches didn't have services on Thursday night when we did, so these families came to our Thursday night meetings. This was during World War II when gasoline was rationed. One of the leading men of one of these other churches lived across the street from me.

He came to me, and said, "Brother Hagin, because of the gasoline rationing, instead of driving all the way to our church, we'd like to start coming to your church. After all, your church is just across the street and we can just walk over."

I said to him, "No, don't join my church. They need you in your own church because you're one of the main board members. They need your support and your finances, especially right now because they are in a building program."

You see, the Bible says we are to consider our brother before ourselves. Besides, I'm not a sheep thief.

Soon after that, some of the members of my church board said to me, "Brother Hagin, these folks who go to those other churches live close to the parsonage. You ought to try to get them to join our church. It would really help us financially."

I said, "Men, I'm not a sheep thief. I'm not going to steal another man's sheep."

Now don't misunderstand me. These people belonged to Full Gospel churches. If they had belonged to some ole dead church which taught that speaking in tongues and divine healing are of the devil, that would have been a different matter.

In a case like that, I would not have refused someone who wanted to come to hear the *full* gospel of the Lord Jesus Christ. And it would have been walking in love to do so. Otherwise, they may never find out about their covenant rights in Christ.

Finally, another one of the men who lived by the parsonage came to me and said, "Brother Hagin, my wife and I want to join your church."

I knew this man only occasionally went to one of those neighboring churches. I told him, "You talk to your pastor about it, and I'll talk to him too. If it's all right with him, and he recommends you, I'll take you. But otherwise, I won't, because I'm not a sheep thief."

I talked to their pastor, and he said, "Brother Hagin, I'm going to insist that you take that family."

I said, "You know I'm not after your sheep."

He said, "Yes, I know that. But, really, for the husband's sake, I'd like you to take this family. He rarely comes here to church. His wife is one of the best workers in my church, and it will be a sacrifice to lose her. But maybe you can influence her husband to walk with God. I believe you can help him. For his sake, I'd like you to take them."

This pastor had that man's best interests at heart. And, thank God, God showed me how to help that man, and he and his wife became a real blessing to the church. But the point I'm trying to make is that ministers need to learn something about not only *Christian* ethics, but also about *ministerial* ethics.

Let me give you another example of ministerial ethics. After I went out in field ministry, over a seven-year period of time, I held five meetings for a certain pastor in a large city. In the course of time, another pastor asked me to come to the same city and hold a meeting for him. I hadn't been back to that first church in two years, and it was a large city.

But I want to be ethical and walk in love in every situation, so I contacted Brother Braun, the pastor of the first church where I'd held the meetings. I wanted to prefer him and put him first and not cause a problem between pastors in a city.

I telephoned Brother Braun and said, "Brother Braun, I've preached for you a number of times over the years. Recently, another pastor in your city has asked me to hold a meeting for him. I feel led to go if it's all right with you."

Even if I had felt led to go to this other church, if this pastor had said, "Don't go," I wouldn't have gone.

I'm not going to create division and strife in a city among pastors. But I knew this pastor was a man of God, and he encouraged me to go.

He said, "Brother Hagin, that pastor is a fine man of God. If you feel led to go, go right ahead. We'll come over and help you."

Who told me to practice that kind of ministerial courtesy? The Holy Spirit dwelling on the inside and the Word of God. The Bible says we are to be doers of the Word and prefer our brother before ourselves.

You see, I had gone to that first church a number of times over a seven-year period. Probably as many as half of his members were saved in the revivals I held for him. If I had come to that city to preach in another church, half of his congregation may have come to hear me. That might have caused problems, or he might have lost some of his people because of it.

This was a large city, and these churches were far enough away from each other that it would have been all right. But on the other hand, we ought to have respect for fellow ministers and fellow members of the Body of Christ and not just run roughshod over one another.

I don't mean I practiced this kind of ministerial courtesy just one time. I've followed that practice over the years in my field ministry because I want to be ethical in all my dealings in the ministry.

I've seen some ministers hold a meeting one week in a church and go almost across the street and start another meeting for someone else! And it created confusion and division in a city and strife between pastors.

I've also seen associate pastors divide a church over some issue and then take half of the congregation two or three blocks away and start another church! That's unethical. Ministers of the gospel shouldn't divide sheepfolds.

That's the reason even some folks in the world don't believe in ministers and have lost faith in the church. Some ministers have created much havoc and confusion, dividing churches and spiritually killing little lambs. If associate pastors or church members can't go along with the way a church is run, then they should leave the church. But they don't need to create division in doing so.

Some ministers who divide churches, say, "The Lord told me . . ." Don't lay that off on the Lord! He's not that way. Some people try to get out of the wrong things they do by using the excuse, "The Lord told me to do it." The Lord never told anyone to be a sheep thief or to divide a church.

I'll tell you the truth about the matter. If ministers live right and do right, people will believe in them. There is nothing more lacking in the Charismatic Movement than commitment, consecration, and respect for the things of God. Ministers of the gospel need to have such integrity that they refuse to do anything that would compromise the gospel they preach.

Pastors shouldn't teach their church members to proselyte members from other churches, saying, "You ought to come to our church. We've got so much more of the Holy Ghost than anyone else." Pastors, just as any other minister, need to be above reproach even in how they get new members.

Some pastors spend all their time trying to get other church members from neighboring churches. Any pastor who does that is a sheep thief. Instead of doing that, he should initiate church programs that reach out to the unsaved and the unchurched!

I know an evangelist who held a meeting for a particular pastor. Every year he came to this pastor's church and held a meeting for him. The church membership doubled under this evangelist's ministry.

One day this evangelist came to the pastor and said, "I'm going to start a church nearby using your members, Brother So-and-so's members, and Brother So-and-so's members."

This evangelist built on the labor of other ministers. He was a sheep thief. I watched that evangelist's ministry. Even though he was in his thirties, within four years, he was dead. He didn't judge himself, so God had to judge him. The Bible says, *"For if we would judge ourselves, we should not be judged"* (1 Cor. 11:31). It is a serious matter to hurt the Body of Christ by unethical practices.

I've been in the ministry more than fifty years. I've watched preachers — pastors, evangelists, teachers — *ministers of the gospel,* climb up over the ministry and reputation of others trying to get to the top in Christian circles.

I've had people try to climb up spiritually by using me and my name too. Doing that is nothing short of a lie. People who do that will eventually fail because they are not building on the Word; they are basing their ministries and reputations on a lie. And they are not being ethical.

Let's just endeavor to prepare ourselves so we can fulfill God's purpose for each of our lives. First, let's prepare our hearts in the Word and by waiting before God in prayer. The Bible promises that those who seek the Lord with all their heart shall find Him. By consecrating and dedicating ourselves for the Master, He can use us to be a blessing to the Body of Christ and to the world.

Prophetic Utterance

There are certain people even in the ministry, including ministers' wives, who have been used to some extent in the area of the gifts of the Spirit. But then they missed it in a few places, they got hurt, and they said, "I'll never do that again."

But the Spirit of God is saying to stir up the gift that is in you and put aside that hurt, and just purpose, "I'll not miss it next time." And as you walk in the Spirit and operate in the Spirit, others will begin to believe in you, and you'll be blessed in your doing. And even those round about you will come to see, and say "Surely the Holy Ghost is manifesting Himself through them."

And then there are those for whom past mistakes, failures, and even sins have numbed your spirit, so to speak. And even some who are in the ministry have thought, *I'll not operate in this area of ministry anymore. People won't have confidence in me.*

But thus saith the Lord: The past is gone and should be forgotten. The blood of Jesus cleanses from all sin, and I look upon you as though you never did anything wrong.

So stir up the gift, and in some occasions, gifts that are within you by the anointing and unction of the Holy Ghost upon you, and begin again to yield to the Holy Spirit. And you will find that as you yield to the Spirit, and as you minister under that anointing, you'll come back to that same level where you were in the Spirit, and you'll go on from there.

And it will seem as though there is a double portion of the Spirit upon you. And men will look upon you and marvel and say, "Oh, the wondrous grace of God." And I'll get all the glory, saith the Lord, and not man. So the work of God shall be accomplished in the earth.

And if it could be told you some of the things that will happen in some of your ministries, you would almost turn aside in unbelief and say, "That couldn't possibly be so." But as you are faithful and walk with Me and learn to walk with the flow of the Holy Spirit, it will surely come to pass. All those round about you shall know you are My beloved, equipped by the Spirit, called of God, and qualified to carry forth the good news to the world.

So rejoice and be glad for there is about to break upon the earth through My Body, which is the Church, a glorious harvest which shall be reaped, and a glorious move of the Spirit. So the work of God shall be accomplished, and there shall be much cause for rejoicing.

*********** **Prayer of Consecration** ***********

Say this from your heart as a prayer of dedication and consecration:

Father, I purpose in my heart to yield to the Holy Ghost, to be motivated by the Spirit of God, and to be regulated by the Word of God. For the Word and the Spirit must agree.

I purpose in my heart to learn how to flow with the Holy Ghost. If the anointing is not there to minister by the gifts of the Spirit, I will go ahead and share the Word, and leave the results with God.

When the anointing comes, I'll be faithful to speak and minister under the unction of the Holy Spirit as He directs. And as I consecrate and dedicate myself to God and His Word, I will allow the Lord Jesus Christ, the Head of the Church, to set me in my place in the Body of Christ to minister as He desires and chooses.

Father, I purpose in my heart to minister and live in such a way that will never bring reproach on the Name of Jesus. I will lift up the Name of Jesus and endeavor to be a blessing to others, not desiring my own glory or that my name or ministry should be magnified. I ask that in everything I do, Jesus Christ receive the glory and the praise. Amen.